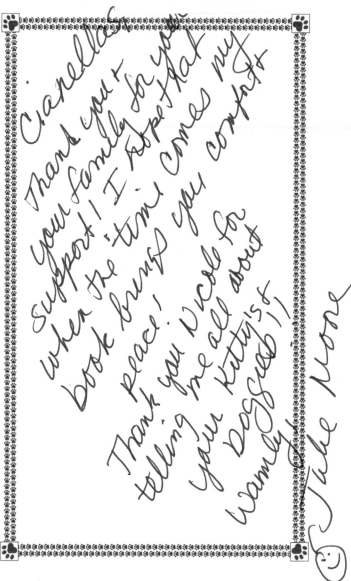

Ciarella +
Thank you +
your family so you
support! I hope that
when the time comes my
book brings you comfort
peace!
Thank you Nicole for
telling me all about
your Kathy 1st
Dog Grab!)

Warmly,

Julie Mone

The Pet Soul Book

A Guide for Letting Go and Connecting with Your Beloved Pet

Julie Moore

Cover Illustration by Cheryl Caro

Gratitude to Dr. Alice Villalobos and Wiley-Blackwell for
permission to reprint the Quality of Life scale; to Martin Scot
Kosins for permission to reprint "The Fourth Day"; and to
Leigh Hester for permission to reprint "Old Dogs Don't Die."

Printed in the United States of America

First Printing, 2020

ISBN-13: 978-1-947637-11-5 print edition
ISBN-13: 978-1-947637-12-2 ebook edition

DreamSculpt Books and Media
An imprint of
Waterside Productions
2055 Oxford Ave
Cardiff, CA 92007
www.DreamSculpt.com

To those wonderful and beloved pet friends I have loved deeply and who have made their transition to spirit-beings before me: Max, Poppy, Honey, Brandy, Sammy, Marty, Misty, Bandit, Sophie, Bryanna, Paco, Pistachio, Jaymo, Moselle, Flash and Cooper. To my loving girl Willow, who is no longer physically with me but still in the physical.

Table of Contents

Author's Note

Do you believe your pet has a soul? If so, this book is for you. What you hold in your hands is intended to be a gift. A gift to yourself or from a loving friend who knows you have just experienced the loss of your pet. If you're not sure if your pet has a soul, this book will lead you closer to more clarity about the meaning of life (which, in my opinion is to experience more joy; after all that's what our beloved pets bring to us!)

I believe that you were given or discovered this book because the messages and ideas within it will resonate with you. In addition to the supportive text, you will find that after each chapter you are provided a mini workbook that has been created for you to practice, reflect on, and bring you more peace. In the back of the book you'll find a scrapbook and journal area to chronicle your journey with your pet. It's a place for a special photo, ideas for rituals and for treasuring any experiences of or signs from your lost pet. Photos of pets featured in this book can also be found on the websites: Juliemooreauthor. com and Thepetsoulbook.com.

After each chapter you can work through your grief using the workbook prompts and questions. I suggest that you put your workbook entries aside after completing them, and then revisit them in a couple of weeks to add to them and see how your grief abates and your new connection with your pet grows.

Don't Weep for Me

Don't weep for me. I now can be free of
all the pain and trouble you see.
I know you're sad and miss me so. But
I'm in your heart, I didn't go.
Just close your eyes and I'll be there,
lying next to your favorite chair.
I'm the warm summer breeze you
feel against your knees
and the soft rustle you hear in the trees.
I'll be there right by your side. My body
is gone but my love never died.
I'll be with you always until that day when
we journey together in heaven's way.

—Ken Johnson, 2003

Introduction

"I'm so sorry for your loss." We all say it to each other after having heard that someone's beloved pet has passed into non-physical (or as most say, has died) or we hear it from someone attempting to console us. But what if it really isn't true? The loss I mean.

Now, I know that most of us <u>feel</u> like we've "lost" our pet, but what if we could think of it in a different way and in a way that soothes the way we feel? After all, our thoughts influence our feelings, so what if the pain, sadness and anguish of the feeling of our pet's having been "lost" could be replaced more gently and quickly with feelings of hope, nostalgia and closeness and we would have the ability to remember them with sweet memories? What if you could lessen the severity and length of your grieving?

As a counselor, the first thing that I want to tell you is that your feelings and emotions are normal. You are not crazy or weird because you loved your pet, in some ways like a child. All of your feelings and emotions are valid, but there could be another way to get through this. I am also not suggesting that you deny or avoid your pain or bypass the grieving process. However, you can "choose to focus on those aspects of your pet that you loved and appreciated,"[1] so that you can move more quickly through the grieving process.

My spirituality has kept me very grounded through the grieving process, as I believe that *we are spiritual beings having a human experience,* and that we are here after death in a different form. This thought has sustained and comforted me, and although sad at times, I am hopeful for the future, have a feeling of peace to comfort me, and can still feel moments of joy even while grieving.

When the idea of this book first manifested itself, I listened to the stories of many friends whose pets had died, some in the distant past and some in the recent past. What I noticed was the severity of their feelings of loss and pain. For most it appeared to be lasting a very long time. These folks appeared to be having a difficult time moving on from their painful feelings of grief. I had just lost two pets in a relatively short amount of time and was at a place where I felt their physical loss, but I had been able to let go of the pain of their deaths much more quickly. This book is for those seeking peace and comfort after their pet passes, and to be able to learn, with an open mind, a way to deeply connect with their pet after its passing.

Now faith is the substance of things hoped for, the evidence of things not seen.

—Hebrews 11:1-3

Chapter 1

Vacancy: Missing My Friend

Moselle and Flash were my old guys of my six basset hounds. At 11 and 12, they got to stay in the house while the four others stayed in the comfortable climate-controlled inside/outside kennel when I was away during the day at work as a high school counselor. I couldn't wait to come home from work and see their sweet faces greet me by the windows on either side of the front door. I would drive up, walk to the door, walk in, and then came their "dance of joy." They jumped very excitedly, barked, twirled around and acted as if they hadn't seen me in years!

After I'd gotten settled a few minutes later, I'd see Moe lying on her back, legs up in the air and head off to the side of the ottoman in the living room. It was like she was beckoning me to come and rub her belly. Moselle was also the instigator of the "hound chorus." She would start baying, and then all the other hounds would join in—all in the living room. Yes, I would even join in. Arrrroooo! We would all bay together and it was so joyful!

Flash was my vocal one. He would always "tell" me what was going on, like when he needed to go out, when it was time for breakfast, and even when it was bedtime. I mean he would *really* tell me. He'd stand right in front of me and vocalize like he was carrying on a conversation. I would say to him, "Tell me about it buddy," or, "…and then what happened Flash?" Basset hounds typically bay or bark, but Flash really "talked" to me. I even tried to teach him to say, "I love you," like in some of those YouTube videos.

I was eventually able to get him to say a version of "go out!" and I would have actual conversations with him. After the death of my husband, Paul, in 2014, I felt less sad and lonely because Flash and Moe were there. When I was grieving Paul's death, they were there to hold, love on and cry with. In time, and over the course of several months, those sweet moments were getting fewer and more far between. I began to see both Moe and Flash decline as they both slowed down and didn't have the spark they once did.

It was a really tough day. You know those days when everything doesn't go the way you think it should. Murphy's Law? As a school counselor, anything can happen on the job and this day was incredibly difficult. I had to do a suicide assessment with one student. I have had to do them much too often lately, and it's one of the most heart-wrenching things to do. I also received a call from an angry parent wondering why their student was getting an

"F" in her English class. I am usually able to defuse a parent's anger by providing some advisement and clarity to the situation and assisting them in reaching the teacher. But on this day, there wasn't anything I could say that would appease them.

However, the relief was that those school experiences, though difficult and painful, kept me distracted from what was really on my heart. I have even told my students that are in crisis that sometimes diving into their schoolwork will provide an almost welcome distraction from their emotional pain of whatever is bothering them.

It was a Monday in the Spring of 2018 and making it that much worse was that over the weekend I had sent my beloved 12-year-old basset hound Flash over "the rainbow bridge." For those of you that may not know the rainbow bridge reference, it's a mythical place that folks will say pets travel over to get to "heaven" after they transition to non-physical or "pass away." It's even said that your pets are waiting for you just over the rainbow bridge, and that's where you will be reunited. If you think that Flash's passing was heart-wrenching, just imagine that the Saturday before I also had to send my 11-year-old beautiful basset Moselle over the rainbow bridge as well. My two sweethearts within seven days. It's really unfathomable. Who experiences that?

As I was driving home, thinking about how I was going to handle the void with both of them gone, tears began welling up. Walking up my porch steps to my house I looked at the windows on either side of the door...nothing. Where were the bookends? The sweet smiling, (yes, they smiled!) barking and quivering-with-joy bodies to greet me every day when I come home?

Oh, the void, there it is. And then I remembered and felt the sadness, emptiness and pain. *Where are they? They are not there. No more, "Come on Moe, come on Flash! Let's go potty!"* I walked in and noticed the quiet. *No, "Tell me what's going on."* No hound chorus, no nails clicking on the vinyl floors, no musty-dog smell, no pee on the floor because they couldn't hold it, no tails going a mile a minute. Just quiet. I sat alone at my dining room table and looked down. There was a void where they were both waiting for me to drop a morsel of food. That also became apparent in the Spring of 2020, when my 11½-year-old basset, Cooper, started acting lethargic and stopped eating.

This was very sudden. He was my new "spokes-puppy"! The one who took over for Flash after he passed and would jump on me to let me know when it was mealtime, and would throw his head back and arrrrooo! He would also bark at me to tell me it was bedtime. He succumbed to a thyroid tumor virtually overnight.

Vet technician, Dina Fantegrossi, poignantly writes, "There is also the matter of the sudden life changes that occur when a pet passes away. There are no more 6 a.m. wet-nosed wake-up calls, daily walks, or warm greetings after a long day at the office. For many people their pets give them a sense of purpose—even a reason for being. When that suddenly vanishes, it is understandably life-altering." [2]

Even now I sometimes experience those past moments as if they are in the present:

I'm alone with my thoughts, and suddenly the quiet allows those sad, lonely, guilty, questioning thoughts. *Oh God, did I do the right thing? Was it really time? Was their quality of life really THAT bad?* I sit down on the couch next to the spot where Flash used to sit and look down at that spot. I don't see anything but feel compelled to speak. "How ya doin' buddy?" I look over at the other couch where Moe used to lie. "Hey Moe, what's goin' on girlfriend?" I desperately want to go over to the couch and nuzzle her and rub her big sweet belly.

I am once again sitting at my dining room table wondering where my spokes-puppy is to tell me that it's time to feed all the dogs their breakfast. I'm talking to the empty spaces and imagining that they are still there. They were there, but now they're not there. Tears begin to well up as I know that they are no longer physically with me. My loves are gone. Those sweet fur bundles of joy and unconditional love are gone. It's heart-wrenching.

I feel my chest begin to heave as I'm crying and grieving, and intellectually I know it's normal, but wonder, *is this feeling okay? Am I crazy to be missing my DOGS this much? They're not people, so I shouldn't be feeling this bad, should I? I MUST be weird!*

I've never had children of my own so my dogs ARE the closest thing that I will have to human children. I desperately missed Flash, Moe, and Cooper's unconditional love. They didn't care if I had bad breath, bed head or that my mascara was smeared from the night before. They just loved me. Now I felt that void and didn't know what to do with those feelings. Having lived with the passing of so many human and canine souls, I've discovered that the hardest human emotion is the grief we feel over the death of someone (human or pet) we have loved.

Missing Your Friend

So, what about you? What is your story? Think back to those memories of your first pet. Remember playing and cuddling them when you were young? You have those memories too of your Buddy, Max, Bella or Ranger. Now think about your first experience with your first pet's death. How did they die? Was it your cat, Rex, that you had since you were born that died of old age? Was it Goldie the goldfish that Mom or Dad flushed down the toilet? How did that feel? Or was it your pet hamster, Chubby, that only lived for two short years? What happened when you learned of their death? Were you there when they died?

Maybe your pet didn't die but was taken from you or given away. In some ways that can feel worse as they are still living but you can't be with them. As a child you may not have had control of the situation. Could it be that your parent never wanted the pet in the first place but you begged them for it, and at the first sign of a problem—they peed on the carpet or chewed on the furniture—they gave your pet away, and you feel like you never got over it?

Do you remember coming home from school or work and not seeing your dog or cat there by the door waiting for you to come home? Maybe their leaving was never even discussed with you, or did you feel supported and understood during this time? What did your folks say, what did your friends say? Were you made fun of for being upset or even devastated? Did someone say to you, "It's only a dog, cat, bird, fish, hamster, etc." and minimize your feelings and make you feel like you were silly for being so upset? What did you do with those feelings? Was there anybody that you felt you could talk to?

This was a significant experience in your life that really mattered. Your relationship with your pet friend may have been the first truly unconditional relationship that you had in your life, and it was important and meaningful to you. Circumstances in your life may have created feelings in you that your pet was the only soul that truly understood you. Your pet may have been your BEST friend; maybe your childhood was traumatic or confusing, and you could only confide in your beloved friend.

When you don't have a loving and supportive environment and people around you who understand your valid feelings surrounding your pet's death, you may find yourself feeling embarrassed about those feelings. You may not get the support you truly need. Even as an adult, you may feel that others really do not understand the depth of your feelings. You may be afraid to share them and stay silent and in emotional pain.

Illustrating this idea is a particularly poignant post on Facebook. I reached out to Wes Thorn, the gentleman who posted it, and he gave me permission to share his thoughts and feelings. He writes, "I don't know if I'm typical of other 50-year-old people. I've been losing friends, family and acquaintances at an alarming rate in the past four years. Every time it happens, I begin to reflect on life. I have grieved the loss of all I have lost, but I must admit, and I admit this with some reluctance, the recent passing that has affected me the most was the loss of my 13-year-old basset, Lincoln, in the summer of 2016. I think it was because he was with me every single day for all my hours at home for so many years. He followed me everywhere, and as good dogs do, he loved his human family members unconditionally."

The experience that Wes shares is more common than we think. Maybe, at least for some, we grieve our pet's death more deeply than even the humans in our lives. Could it be that because of the unconditional nature of our pets' love, more and more of us grieve their passing deeper than some of us are willing to admit? Wes reached out and shared his thoughts on Facebook and maybe those connections with other like-minded folks allowed for greater healing. I am hoping that the following chapters will bring you peace and help you through situations or feelings from past grief, or if you are currently going through those feelings, will help guide you through them.

I Will Wait For You

I came to you late last night
To be with you while you slept
I lay my head on your pillow
While next to me you wept
A gentle smile kissed your lips
As I licked away a tear
Until your time to join me
I'll be waiting through the years.
—Author Unknown

Paw Prints

🐾 Do you have memories of your first pet and how they transitioned to the non-physical realm?

🐾 Do you remember if you had support during that time? Was it helpful or hurtful?

🐾 What have you done to support yourself emotionally during this time?

Workbook for Chapter 1

It's important to feel and experience your
grief, then when it's time, you release
the grief and keep the fond and special
memories without the painful emotions.

Exercise 1 – Write a letter to your pet. Really pour it
out. Let them know how you're feeling i.e., how
the fact that they are no longer here in the physical is affecting you.

Exercise 2 – List all of the qualities that made your
pet special to you. Really clarify your feelings so
that you solidify your memories.

Exercise 3 – Think back about your experience with
your first pet. Tell an understanding friend or
write that story in a journal.

Exercise 4 – Write an online eulogy for your pet.
This will help memorialize your pet and help
you work through some of your grief.

Exercise 5 – Were you ever embarrassed by someone's attitude about your grief over your pet's
death? Write about that experience.

May I Go Now?

May I go now?
Do you think the time is right?
May I say good-bye to pain-filled days
and endless lonely nights?
I've lived my life and done my best,
an example tried to be.
So can I take that step beyond
and set my spirit free?
I didn't want to go at first,
I fought with all my might.
But something seems to draw me now
to a warm and loving light.
I want to go.
I really do.
It's difficult to stay.
But I will try as best I can
to live just one more day
To give you time to care for me
and share your love and fears.
I know you're sad and so afraid,
because I see your tears.
I'll not be far,
I promise that, and hope you'll always know
that my spirit will be close to you,
wherever you may go.
Thank you for loving me.
You know I love you too.
That's why it's hard to say good-bye

and end this life with you.
So hold me now, just one more time
and let me hear you say,
because you care so much for me,
you'll let me go today.

—*Susan A. Jackson*

Chapter 2
When Your Friend is Dying

When my Flash was close to the end of his life, I could see him slowing down, having trouble getting up on "his" sofa, and depending on daily pain medication for arthritis. He was also only intermittently eating. The sweet temperament that was my Flash changed especially toward my other bassets due to his discomfort and likely bouts of real pain, despite my best efforts with the medication. He was even downright mean to my 15-month-old basset puppy.

Moselle's final days were very different. Seven weeks prior to her death she had a cancerous mammary tumor removed and the veterinarian felt like he "got it all." For several weeks after the surgery I felt sure that everything was going to be alright. I really believed it. Sadly, just a few months later I noticed a difference in her. She began declining. In the days near the end she was sleeping all the time, acting lethargic, and hardly eating and drinking.

The experiences leading up to your own pet's passing may be similar; however, they also may be quite different. There is no one specific way that animals behave in their final days and hours.

Recently, at the request of a friend, I counseled her adult daughter when she accidentally closed the door of her car after unloading groceries, and unbeknownst to her, their family dog had jumped into the car. The family did a massive search for the next 24 hours. They discovered him the following day in the car and realized that he had perished the previous day. She shared with me that she felt incredibly responsible and was overwhelmed and overcome with guilt. These real stories of our love and devotion, and the experience of suffering, make it so difficult to fully move on. Just recently I was talking to a friend who said that after experiencing devastating illnesses with her two dogs, she believes that she couldn't bear to have another dog. She feels traumatized by her experience with their death. This book is exactly for such a person. In fact, this book is for everyone who is experiencing grief and feelings of loss.

The Impossible Choice

Your beloved pet, your baby, your number one, your ride or die—is dying … *Oh my God, what do I do?* How do you choose between life and death? When do you know the right time to let them go? How can I possibly make such a difficult and impossible emotional decision? As a pet owner, if you're reading this book you've either been there, are about to be, or in the back of your mind know that you will face that decision one day. It's excruciating, painful, awful and confusing. I felt devastated when it was time to make the decision about Moselle and Flash. It was too cruel and too big a decision to handle on my own.

Martin Scot Kosins said it so beautifully in his short written work, "And on this day, if your friend and God have not decided for you, then you will be faced with making a decision of your own on behalf of your lifelong friend, and with the guidance of your own deepest Spirit. But whichever way your friend eventually leaves you, you will feel as lone as a single star in the dark night." [3] (Full version in the appendix). There are so many end-of-life scenarios, and none of them are easy.

Let me help.

When You and Your Significant Other are Not on the Same Page

Some years ago, when my husband Paul was alive, we had a beagle named Bandit. Paul had asked me to go with him one day to a family's home in our town as he had found out in the newspaper that they had a litter of beagle puppies. At the time I did not know anything about "responsible breeding," that is, breeders who breed to their dog's breed standard and do necessary health testing. I only knew they were classic "backyard breeders" who typically just bred to "have puppies" or just for the money.

Nonetheless they were super cute, and Paul wanted one. We left with our Bandit that afternoon and we absolutely adored him.

Now, most people have seen a finely bred, cute beagle. He wasn't a perfect show dog beagle, and I was pretty sure that he was a mix with coonhound or some sort of other hound because he was BIG. One day a sportsman friend of Paul's saw Bandit and when we asked what breed he thought that he might be, Paul's friend exclaimed enthusiastically, "Oh! Bandit is a big 'ole hunting beagle!" We laughed and laughed, and from that moment on we referred to him as our "big 'ole hunting beagle, Bandit!" I absolutely loved him as he was so loving, loyal and wonderful, but he was also **Paul's** dog.

They played on the floor together, wrestled and always had a blast! They had a very special bond. The years passed and our love for him grew every day. One day when Bandit was only eight years old, we noticed a growth on his chest. Within two to three months it was the size of an orange. We couldn't believe it. How could this happen so quickly and, in a dog so young? When we brought him to the vet, we discovered that he had a type of very aggressive cancer called hemangiosarcoma. At the vet's rec- ommendation we decided to have him operate to remove it. The vet was VERY encouraging and opti- mistic and felt that he'd gotten the entire tumor.

But much to our horror and dismay, about a month later it began to grow back and within four months it was the same size as before the surgery. We were devastated and were told by our vet that any further surgery would be ineffective. So our focus shifted to keeping him as comfortable as possible and loving him fiercely for as long as he had.

The challenge that Paul and I faced was that we were not on the same page with regards to when was the right time to let him go. I really felt that I had to defer to Paul because our Bandit was really his baby. But it was so especially hard for me as we saw him decline, and I was sure that Bandit had at one point given me "the look." He was declining rapidly. He was sleeping all the time and we had him on two pain medications. Paul was waiting for a clearer sign such as no eating or drinking, but Bandit was having trouble getting up, and I was having trouble because I felt that he was more uncomfortable than comfortable. It was a really tough time for all of us. Ultimately, I felt that I had to let Paul make the decision.

My suggestion is that if you find yourself in a similar situation (if you have pets and a significant other, you most certainly will), you will have to make hard decisions and compromises. You may want to talk together about your views on end-of-life issues with your significant other before it comes up and decide ahead of time how you will respond and how you will make the decision together. It still won't be an easy decision and you still may be challenged, but at least you will have had the talk beforehand.

Some Answers: Quality of Life Scale

It's usually the signs that your pet displays that will let you know when you must start thinking about easing and preventing their pain and suffering. I know for me it's seeing a decline that doesn't improve and that begins to affect their quality of life. Something is different, and things that were easy for them no longer are. This decision is usually a heart-wrenching struggle because you want to end your pet's suffering or poor quality of life, but you also want one more month, week, hour or minute with them. When I knew that Flash, Moselle and Cooper were no longer able to live without discomfort, had stopped wanting to eat and play, and had appeared lethargic, I went back-and-forth but eventually, I just knew. It's one of the most difficult decisions that you'll make because there is no clear-cut decision tree. The right time for one of your pets may not be the right time for another one. That's one of the reasons why the question of "when is the right time?" is so challenging. The other challenge is you have such a deep emotional attachment with your pet that your heart screams, *NO, it can't be time yet!* but your head tells you it is.

I can tell you as a counselor that it's important you know and understand that any and every decision or choice you make is the RIGHT one and that there are some helpful tools to help you through this. Start by talking to loving, supportive and UNDERSTANDING pet-loving friends. Share with them your concerns. Let them help you find some clarity in your decision, though always remember that it is YOUR decision. There is also a "Quality of Life Scale" that could be helpful. Using an objective scale can often be helpful in providing additional clarity with this very difficult decision.

Quality of Life Scale (The HHHHHMM Scale)	
Pet caregivers can use this Quality of Life Scale to determine the success of Pawspice care. Score patients using a scale of: 0 to 10 (10 being ideal).	
Score	Criterion
0-10	**HURT** - Adequate pain control & breathing ability is of top concern. Trouble breathing outweighs all concerns. Is the pet's pain well managed? Can the pet breathe properly? Is oxygen supplementation necessary?
0-10	**HUNGER** - Is the pet eating enough? Does hand feeding help? Does the pet need a feeding tube?
0-10	**HYDRATION** - Is the pet dehydrated? For patients not drinking enough water, use subcutaneous fluids daily or twice daily to supplement fluid intake.
0-10	**HYGIENE** - The pet should be brushed and cleaned, particularly after eliminations. Avoid pressure sores with soft bedding and keep all wounds clean.
0-10	**HAPPINESS** - Does the pet express joy and interest? Is the pet responsive to family, toys, etc.? Is the pet depressed, lonely, anxious, bored or afraid? Can the pet's bed be moved to be close to family activities?
0-10	**MOBILITY** - Can the pet get up without assistance? Does the pet need human or mechanical help (e.g., a cart)? Does the pet feel like going for a walk? Is the pet having seizures or stumbling? (Some caregivers feel euthanasia is preferable to amputation, but an animal with limited mobility yet still alert, happy and responsive can have a good quality of life as long as caregivers are committed to helping their pet.)
0-10	**MORE GOOD DAYS THAN BAD** - When bad days outnumber good days, quality of life might be too compromised. When a healthy human-animal bond is no longer possible, the caregiver must be made aware that the end is near. The decision for euthanasia needs to be made if the pet is suffering. If death comes peacefully and painlessly at home, that is okay.
*TOTAL	*A total over 35 points represents acceptable life quality to continue with pet hospice (Pawspice).

Original concept, Oncology Outlook, by Dr. Alice Villalobos, Quality of Life Scale Helps Make Final Call, VPN, 09/2004; scale format created for author's book, Canine and Feline Geriatric Oncology: Honoring the Human-Animal Bond, Blackwell Publishing, 2007. Revised for the International Veterinary Association of Pain Management (IVAPM) 2011 Palliative Care and Hospice Guidelines. Reprinted with permission from Dr. Alice Villalobos & Wiley-Blackwell.

Used with permission. © Alice Villalobos, DVM

This scale, developed by veterinarian Alice Villalobos, DVM, will help you evaluate your pet's current condition and level of challenges. I know it's hard to do when you're so emotionally attached and can't bear to let go. That's why I keep emphasizing getting and having support around your decision. You can also ask your vet to help provide some clarity. One friend told me that her vet helped her by asking three important questions:

1. Do they still greet you at the door?
2. Can/do they get up to eat or drink on their own?
3. Can/do they go to the door on their own to let you know they have to go potty?

If any one of these are a "no," you have your answer.

In my case, I always knew that my pet would, "tell me when it was time." This is especially the case when you have an older pet who may have started to experience discomfort. In Flash's case, I was spending more and more quiet loving time with him, and had even said to him one evening while we were cuddling, "Tell me buddy when you're ready. Let Mama know." One night he gave me the "look," you know what I mean, and I knew it was his time. He looked deeply in my eyes with a soulful and mournful look that seemed to say, "Let me go, I'm ready, Mom. I don't want to go on like this Mom. It hurts too much Mom."

I know that some of you have experienced this with your own beloved pet. A gentleman named Jonathan Chandler wrote a wonderfully loving and touching eulogy on Facebook to his beloved dog Stanley: "For at least a year, I've been telling him that he just needs to let me know. Three days ago, I looked into his eyes, and he told me. There was no question about it."

I have found that most of the time you feel it "in your gut" when you know it's time, even though you really don't want to let go. When I knew the time had come, I mustered up the strength, reached out and got support from loving friends and family who understood that my pet was an extension of me. To me the loss of the physical nature of them is just as painful as a human loss would be. For those people in your life who believe "it's only an animal," I would advise not discussing your pain, your decision-making, or your struggles with those folks, because while you feel and know that your pet was your *baby,* their reactions may be muted and unsupportive, leaving you feeling worse.

I reached out to Carolyn Hodges and Damon LeBlanc, owners of Faithful Friends Pet Cremation in my hometown and they imparted this story about a client. The wisdom it carried, I believe, will be helpful to you. They shared, "A client brought his Chihuahua to us at the end of his life and asked, 'How do you know when the time is right?'" Carolyn told him that your mental/head and emotional/

heart state have to match. "When your mind knows and your heart is telling you it's the right time to do this, you will do it." Carolyn went on to share, "I can remember him because he was so sweet in wanting us to know his dog while he was still physical. The owner wanted us to make an emotional connection with his dog. You love your pet and you don't want it to go, but you've got to get to that place where your head and your heart meet and then you'll know."

Your pet's death process will usually come in one of two ways. They will have a natural death, or you will have to make the decision to put your pet to sleep. I can't tell you how many times I sat next to Flash before going to bed and telling him, "It's okay buddy if you need to go tonight, honey." Of course it wasn't alright, but the alternative of me having to make the decision about when the right time was definitely was not something I wished to face. When I would tell him that, I was secretly HOPING not to have to make that decision. Most of you will come to a point when you have to make the decision to let your baby go—you know that in terms of their suffering, it's always better to be early than even one day too late. Think of it as the most LOVING thing you can do, even if you can't bear the thought of them being physically gone from your life. You are giving your pet the gift of peace, free from the pain and discomfort of life. A recent Facebook post from a dog owner said, "When I researched how people made their decisions regarding end-of-life for their beloved companions, the only regret was they wished they hadn't waited so long to end their suffering. That helped me to put myself in their (pet's) place but it does not make it any easier."

Should you be there?

Deciding to be there at your pet's euthanasia is a highly personal decision. Earlier in my life, my first husband, Bill, and I had purchased a Yorkshire terrier named Sammy from a pet store. Sammy had chronic skin-related health problems throughout his life. We were having to medicate him daily with prednisone, an anti-inflammatory steroid. The veterinarian had cautioned that a young dog on daily prescribed prednisone would likely have organ failure issues at some point, but we just didn't realize that he would be affected at such a young age. Unfortunately, at the young age of seven, we realized that his quality of life was so poor that we had to make the painful decision to let him go.

The decision to put him to sleep felt especially unfair because of his young age, and he was my first dog as an adult. Having to make the decisions for his care without my parents and having to decide to end his life intentionally because of his poor quality of life was particularly difficult. At the time, I couldn't bear the thought of being there to see his last moments, so Bill, by himself, took Sammy to the vet to be euthanized. After Sammy was gone, I had time to think it through, and I really regretted not being there. I remember throwing myself on the bed and crying for several nights, missing him so much and feeling the void from his absence.

Since that time, and after some serious soul searching, I have come to realize that the most loving thing I know I can do is to be there to hold my friend when they take their last physical breath. I never regret that decision. I am now always there with my pet in their final moments. Not being with Sammy at his time of death was a powerful decision, and a lesson for me that I couldn't do over or take back. Now I find that even though terribly painful, being there is an emotional and intimate moment to share with my loved one during their final moments. Holding them at the time they pass into non-physical helps me feel more connected and provides the necessary physical closure that I missed with Sammy. However, this is still a personal decision, and if it is too painful for you, that's alright too. Remember, it's always about whatever works and feels best to you. If you think that you want to be there but need support, bring a trusted family member or friend with you who understands.

I was recently talking to my dear friends Amy and Pat Siniscalchi on FaceTime. As I was sharing the premise of this book, they relayed a beautiful story about their final moments with their beloved pug, Wilbur. Amy mentioned that Wilbur appeared to be experiencing a lot of emotional and psychological pain in the days leading up to his death which manifested by him crying out, or just standing in the middle of the room and staring off at a wall or at nothing at all. They knew these were signs of possible pain, but also certainly signs of tremendous anxiety.

Wilbur just wasn't acting as he normally would, and they knew that the end of his physical life was near. Amy said, "He just wasn't himself. He wasn't our Wilbur." Amy and Pat asked their vet to come to their home for a home euthanasia. They told me that it was important to them to say goodbye at home. However, as with many stories I've heard and personally experienced, Wilbur was having a bit of a "good day" the morning that they chose to say goodbye. Amy had said to Pat, "Maybe it's not time, he's having such a good day." Pat then replied, "Wouldn't you want your last day to be a good one?" That sentiment really helped Amy be okay with the decision that they had made. She wanted Wilbur to have a good last day. She said, "I didn't want to put him through more pain just because it's hard to say goodbye." The vet first administered some Valium to calm him. Amy said the next thing that happened was remarkable. As he calmed, the light came back to his eyes and Amy exclaimed, "It was him! I FELT him and I saw HIM again! He had a few moments of clarity, and it was such a gift. I looked at him and said, 'There HE is!'" It was then that she and Pat felt that Wilbur could understand and hear them as they said their last goodbyes. They were able to tell him that they loved him and that he was such a good boy. Their story reinforced how important it can be to be with your loved one in their final moments and to allow them to give you that gift of love and connection, even in spite of tremendous sadness.

I came across a particularly moving eulogy written on a veterinarian's website memorial page. Loving pet owner, Sam Jojola, wrote about the moments preceding his beloved dog Shiner's passing to non-physical:

"Sue and I placed Shiner's favorite toys next to him as I read a series of Bible verses with Sue. Shiner was listening. We lit candles and opened our slider to the Pacific breezes that he loved so much and had shared with us for over a decade. Our dear friend Alexa brought Chelsea, Shiner's 13-year-old friend and walking companion canine for 8 years to say goodbye for the last time and left a beautiful flower next to Shiner's face before departing. I burned a special root given to me by a Pueblo medicine man in my youth. I removed a sage bundle from a medicine bag a Lakota healer gave me years ago. I played John Hulling's 'Breath of the Mountain' from YouTube that reminded me of my wilderness backpacking days where I found comfort in the remote solitude and felt the powerful presence of our Creator.

"As if by magic, our laptop screen switched to Liquid Mind – My Orchid Spirit (Extragalactic). What a coincidence that Shiner had laid next to a phalaenopsis orchid we had next to his bed before he passed on that I bought for Sue on Mother's Day.

"It was profoundly telepathic.

"Somehow, the song 'Come to Me' by Hiroshima entered my thoughts. I had not heard this song for many years. Only when we listened to the words that the message was so overwhelmingly powerful, and our tears would not stop...

"It was as though Shiner was comforting us at that moment in a way we would know.

"It was very powerfully mystical and spiritual...

"Two weeks to the day he passed, Sue was looking through some family photos and stumbled on a photo that I took in October, 2005 depicting Shiner with his then canine companion, Chipper, a mischievous Chowpit mix that an owner let run for hours a day off leash with Shiner in Northern California where I lived.

"I could never find that photo whenever I looked for it."

When I heard Sue and Sam's Shiner's story, this quote came to mind. "The greatest experience we can have is the mysterious." – Albert Einstein (1879-1955).

I was so moved by this story that I felt compelled to speak to Sam about the experience. I reached out to him and when we spoke, Sam wanted me to know and to share that it was so important to have Shiner surrounded by the people and things that meant the most to him. The family wanted to utilize all of their senses, so they lit candles, recited scripture, played special music and burned sage to create a loving memory at the end of Shiner's physical life. Now they can look back knowing that they honored him and themselves with this moving end-of-life experience. This wake-ritual also provided context for connection experiences that Sam shared he and his family had later on.

This story illustrates that **your** pet's end of physical life can be intimate, moving, beautiful, and that you too can create a poignant memory, one that is special and unique for you and your pet. It can be a special "wake-like" atmosphere with your pet's favorite toys and anything that you feel would be meaningful i.e., candles, music and scents to create the mood for your family. Shiner's family chose an in-home euthanasia, and their veterinarian made a house call. This was particularly important to them, and you might consider it as well.

Guilt

Let's talk about guilt. In addition to the grief for your loss, guilt about any part of your pet's death process is the next most difficult thing. I want to say again, any decision you make to end your loving pet's suffering is the right one. When I was trying to make Moselle's end-of-life decision, it was compounded by the fact that I knew Flash's end was near as well. I knew that I could probably eke out a few more days with her, but I could see that she was fading, was uncomfortable, and just like Flash, had also given me "the look." I'll never forget, I was on the floor with her as she no longer felt good enough to jump up on the ottoman (which was her favorite place to sleep). Petting her and crying, she looked up at me with her soulful eyes. I just knew that she was telling me her time was near. Although I was so sad, I knew I had to respect her wishes...she was my FRIEND and LOVED ONE. How could I not? However, even with all of that I still felt pangs of guilt. *Is it too soon? Should I wait a few more days?* I had to decide. Looking in her eyes and seeing what I guessed about the level of her suffering, I knew I had to do it soon.

I had been consoling a family that had made a very difficult decision to put their beloved dog, Paco, down. Paco was a dog that I had personally bred six years before. This wonderful family was a dream home for a breeder. A sweet, loving, dedicated, committed, professional couple that would do anything for their dog. They were such a good home that I ultimately gave them his littermate, Sammy. They loved their sweet tan and white bassets.

After a year of having him, Paco began to exhibit some strange and shocking symptoms. He had become intermittently and unpredictably aggressive, which is very unusual behavior for a basset hound. Bassets typically have sweet temperaments as their breed standard dictates. They tried everything to treat his illness, medically, behaviorally and pharmaceutically, for six long years. They spent thousands of dollars and drove many miles and consulted countless experts to attempt any treatment that might be effective. They even delayed a much-wanted kitchen remodel as they spent the money on Paco. They also put off having their first child for several years. That might seem surprising, but this is how much they loved him and how committed to him they were.

They were always consulting me and wanted me to be kept abreast of all that they were trying. I appreciated it because as a responsible heritage-preservation breeder (a breeder who health-tests, breeds to the breed standard, and commits to advise and assist the families of their puppies for life), it was important for me to continue to support them throughout Paco's life and especially through this difficult time. After some research we realized that Paco had what was likely a condition called "rage syndrome." I had never before heard of a basset hound having the condition. They continued to share what they were doing every step of the way. We discussed many options over many years. There was much discussion, thought, and back and forth decision-making about the possibility of euthanizing him as his quality of life began to deteriorate, but they wouldn't have it at the time, so they tried to change and modify their lifestyle around his needs.

In 2018 they discovered that they were pregnant. Shortly after, they had their first child and were thrilled. I was too, but I was also scared of the

potential for Paco to harm their baby due to his condition. Prior to their baby's birth they took thoughtful steps to ensure the infant's safety. They spent
months making plans and arranging their home
with safety in mind. They had to sequester Paco to a
different part of the house because of the baby.

Paco's condition began to deteriorate as did
his quality of life, so ultimately, after many years
of treatments and plans, they agonized, but finally
made the painful decision to put him to sleep after
a frightening incident that could have harmed their
child. It was gut-wrenching. They were afraid of the
judgements that some might have about their very
personal decision. But because of Paco's deteriorat-
ing quality of life, and the effort it took to attend
to his many needs, those became the reasons that
caused them to make the decision that they felt they
had to make.

The guilty feelings they have had and shared
with me were so painful to hear. Paco had become
dangerous for their family and his quality of life
had deteriorated as well. Their grief was especially
painful because Paco's special needs controlled and
drove every decision that they made. After Paco's
transition into non-physical, they realized that the
day-to-day challenges with him and the fact he was
no longer physically with them, created such a void
in their lives even though his condition and needs
were so difficult. I helped them see that his quality
of life was so compromised. It was also important for

me to counsel them that he was still spiritually with them, and even though they can no longer see him, they may be able to feel his presence.

A big part of this grief is that our pets are vessels of unconditional love. They know we love them, and they show us their love all of the time, even in times when they are ill. As humans we rarely experience true unconditional love from each other, but we do from our pets and when they transition to non-physical, we miss that day-to-day genuine interaction with them.

Author Dean Koontz writes, "No matter how close we are to another person, few human relationships are as free from strife, disagreement, and frustration as is the relationship you have with a good dog. Few human beings give of themselves to another as a dog gives of itself. I also suspect that we cherish dogs because their unblemished souls make us wish—consciously or unconsciously—that we were as innocent as they are and make us yearn for a place where innocence is universal and where the meanness, the betrayals, and the cruelties of this world are unknown." [4]

Guilt Over Financial Challenges

Another situation you may find yourself in is that gut-wrenching and seriously guilt-producing time when your financial situation impacts your decisions. You may experience a crisis when your vet tells you your pet needs life-saving surgery, expensive treatments (think cancer), or ongoing expensive drug therapy, and you know it is beyond your financial means. You certainly can try all means to raise the money from family, help from crowdfunding sites, credit cards or the Care Credit Card (a credit card that can be used for routine or emergency veterinary services and typically can be applied for and approval received on the spot). But that may not solve the problem or raise the significant money you may need. You could try a low-cost vet clinic or offer to make payments for treatment.

Now could be the time to start researching pet insurance, especially for that catastrophic situation "just in case," but at some point, you may just have to make the decision to let your pet go. Just know that even though you are experiencing tremendous guilty feelings, you are doing the very best you can with what you have at the time, and you can work through your guilt with a trusted pet friend, family member or in some cases a pet or traditional therapist. Remember, that any and every decision and choice you make is the only one that matters and will be the right one for your situation.

How to Forgive Yourself

Earlier I mentioned the young woman whose dog jumped into their car and was accidentally closed inside. She was devastated and guilt stricken. As a counselor I am often charged with helping people move through guilt to forgiveness. Some of the hardest work is helping people deal with their own forgiveness issues for themselves. Why is it that we can get to a place of forgiving others, but doing the same for ourselves is so difficult? We are extremely self-critical, continually judging ourselves and yet sharing meme's on Facebook, Twitter, Instagram and Snapchat to "be good to each other," "forgive others," etc.

I believe it's also imperative that we all start with working on our ability to love and forgive ourselves. As a loving pet parent/owner, we would do and give almost anything to show our friend love, connection and compassion. We come from a place of good intent. When situations and decisions surface that cause us to take action on behalf of our pet, those circumstances force us to have to choose the better of two difficult decisions. We cannot always help the fact that we don't have the necessary resources to provide for, or take care of, our pet in the way that we would ultimately love to, but we do the best we can with what we have at the time. Sometimes we can also ask for help and get it, but often others are unable to help.

When I was going through the painful decision about whether or not I could afford to pay for a life-saving surgery to save my 16-month old puppy in the summer of 2018 (with only a 50 percent chance of survival), I agonized over it. Of course, I wanted to spare no expense! I had already spent several hundred dollars and now it was going to be thousands. Not everybody has the resources to move forward and are faced into having to choose not to. I didn't have all the resources at the time. But I was fortunate that my loving friend Kathy was keeping in touch with me through this all. Upon hearing about my plight, she came forward and offered to help me financially. She said, "You will not make this decision because of money." I was lucky that time, and gratefully accepted her help. I also found joy in paying her back and sending a unique basset hound card each time with the monthly repayment checks. Sometimes a friend will come forward, but you have to know that most times you will be on your own.

Paw Prints

* Can you identify certain signs that it is the right time to let your pet go?
* Do you have a process in place to work through if you're ready to let your pet go, however your partner is not ready?
* Can you accept that any decision you make regarding your pet's end is the right one?

Workbook for Chapter 2

Exercise 1 – Make a list of the questions that you will ask yourself in order to get clarity around your pet's "time."

Exercise 2 – Prior to the end of your pet's physical life, begin to formulate decisions around how you will pay for your pet's treatment or medications. Write those down.

Exercise 3 – Research pet insurance companies and a Care Credit Card or begin a special pet savings account and commit to transferring a specified amount into that account every month.

Crossing Over

Oh, please don't feel guilty
It was just my time to go.
I see you are still feeling sad,
And the tears just seem to flow.
We all come to earth for our lifetime,
And for some it's not many years
I don't want you to keep crying
You are shedding so many tears.
I haven't really left you
Even though it may seem so.
I have just gone to my heavenly home,
And I'm closer to you than you know.
Just believe that when you say my
name, I'm standing next to you,
I know you long to see me, But
there's nothing I can do.
But I'll still send you messages
And hope you understand,
That when your time comes to "cross over,"
I'll be there to take your hand.
—Author Unknown

Chapter 3
The Power of Grief

What If Your Grief Doesn't Have to Last a Long Time?

Grief takes many forms and there are many circumstances in which you may experience it with your pets. Certainly, anticipating your pet's death through euthanasia would be one such situation, or their natural death, but it can also take the form of causing your own pet's death through an accident or even experiencing their loss through a relationship break-up (think divorce or breeder/and co-ownership break-up for folks in the dog, cat or horse show world). You may be volunteering at a shelter, pet fostering, or show handling where you may get very attached to a pet and have to give them up, give them back to their owner or place them in a new home. All of these experiences can cause profound feelings of grief.

It is important to honor your grief and to recognize the normal feelings that are typically associated with it. Remember, if you had a significant pet in your life when you were a child, let's say age five or six, and the average age of that pet when it transitioned is 10 to 13 years, you could have six or seven pets in your lifetime. That's six or seven times or more if you have multiple pets that you would experience grief. So, it makes sense to try to find a different way of thinking to ease the pain and sorrow of your pet's eventual death. There may even be a significant improvement in the way you grieve and process the significant human deaths that you experience by embracing a new way of thinking.

As a counselor, I often assist a pet owner in developing emotional awareness and not feeling that there is something wrong because they have a profound reaction to the physical loss of their pet. Think back to when you had your first pet. It may have been a dog, cat, bird or horse. Maybe it was a lizard, rabbit, hamster, guinea pig or fish. Do you remember how old you were when your beloved first pet died? How did you react, and also importantly, how did your support system react to your loss?

I think back to when I was a little girl and we got our first dog, a handsome grey schnauzer named Max. It never occurred to me at that age that Max would ever die. As a young girl it felt like we had a whole lifetime ahead of us. He and I had a very special relationship, and at the time it almost seemed that he was a "person trapped in a dog's body." We connected on a different level and I could "talk" to him. He was thirteen and I was in college at the time of his death. I was devastated.

To help you normalize your feelings of grief it is important to be reassured about what is "normal." This is especially true when it comes to the physical loss of your pet as we don't always understand the severity of our feelings. Thankfully, in 1990, Dr. Wallace Sife, who founded the Association for Pet Loss and Bereavement, developed seven stages that people typically experience when they are "intensely bonded with their pet." Knowing these stages will help you normalize your experience. Those stages of bereavement after physical pet loss are: shock and disbelief; anger; alienation and distancing; denial; guilt; depression; and resolution. They do not have to be sequential but Dr. Sife believes that "shock and disbelief are almost always the first ones."

Please remember that you need to take all the time you need to move through your grief, and in no way should you bypass this important human process as it is a natural expression of physical loss. However with that said, Mary Morrissey (a leader in the human potential movement), advises, "you don't want to pitch your tent there." Life is supposed to be fun, joyful, rich and meaningful, and quite frankly I do not believe your pet would want you to spend months, or in some cases years, in grief and sorrow over their death. Your pet was there to bring you joy, and they would want their memory for your times together to bring you joy as well. It's important to attempt to shift away from those thoughts of missing and loss and to move to appreciation and gratitude for the life you had together, to remember the wonderful love and experiences you shared. I wish that I had known this when Max passed away. Helen Keller said, "What we have once enjoyed deeply we can never lose. All that we loved deeply becomes a part of us." I love this beautiful sentiment by Ms. Keller. It truly embodies the message of this book.

The hard part is we know in our heart that our pet will die one day, but for some reason when it gets closer to that time it's almost like we go into a state of denial. We feel "there's no way that mine is going to die. Mine will live forever." The reason is that there is an unusually deep and wonderful relationship that is unconditional on the pet's behalf.

I believe that it is possible to move through the grieving process more quickly if you want to and if you are ready to be open to the possibility of experiencing a feeling of nostalgia versus gut-wrenching pain. However, you may not want to, or be ready for, the grieving to end and that's okay. But if you would like quicker relief, I challenge you to stay open and continue with me.

One of the truths that I believe we've forgotten is the idea of the circle of life. Death is a part of life and because everybody dies, and every pet dies it isn't a unique experience. Collins English Dictionary describes the concept as: "Nature's way of taking and giving back **life** to earth. It symbolizes the universe being sacred and divine. It represents the infinite nature of energy."

Author of the famous book *On Death and Dying*, Elisabeth Kübler-Ross writes, "It might be helpful if more people would talk about death and dying as an intrinsic part of life just as they do not hesitate to mention when someone is expecting a new baby." [5] It doesn't make the reality of our pet's death and the accompanying grief go away, but that small shift in thought can perhaps lessen the severity of it. Everyone who has ever had a pet, walks through this journey of grief and the feeling of loss of the physical experience with their beloved friend. You will miss the physical presence of your pet, however their spiritual presence will always be right there with you. This idea is beautifully captured by Richard Bach: "What the caterpillar calls the end of the world, the master calls a butterfly." [6]

Remember, the degree, length of time, and depth of your grieving does not equal the degree of your love for your pet. Let me challenge some conventional thinking here: Who came up with that? Who says that this view has anything to do with how much you loved that beautiful soul that was with you? What if your pet's death is a catalyst for a new desire and ability to see signs and allow you to communicate differently with them? To me that shows more love, not how deeply or how long you have to suffer.

To be honest, I initially questioned this myself. I had to work through it as I became concerned that if it appeared that I just "got over" the grief of Flash and Moselle's death too easily, it meant that I didn't care or truly love them. I think sometimes we are afraid we will forget our pet if we don't have the energy and feelings of grief strongly around us. Know that the bond with your pet can never be, and will never be, broken. I also feared judgments from others who believe that grieving for a long time is necessary to prove the extent of our love, and that if I am able to get over it so quickly what does that say about the depth of my compassion, empathy and love for my pet?

During a recent weekend at a dog show, I met a couple whose beloved basset hound had transitioned the year before. The woman was still having a tremendously difficult time with her continuing feelings of loss. She was still openly grieving and expressed that she was continuing to suffer. She even mentioned that she didn't know if she could stay and watch the bassets at ringside, as it would be too painful. You could see in her husband's eyes how concerned he was for her. I later discovered how much he hoped that she would be able to move through her feelings.

Even though I was just about to go into the show ring, I was able to spend a short time talking and counseling her. I reminded her that she had come to the show for a reason. It was to celebrate the basset hound and her time with her basset girl. She was also there to honor her basset. The woman became emotional, and I told her it was okay to cry. All of the basset hound exhibitors around the show ring spoke to her, encouraged and comforted her. Some of us even asked her to hold the leads of our other dogs while we were in the ring. There was a real out-pouring of love and support for her from all of us. These are feelings we all have or will experience. As she began to interact with our bassets, she appeared to be experiencing more joy. We began to see her smile. We could also see how relieved her husband looked.

The following day of the show we were getting ready at the ring again. The same couple came and walked up to us. The woman told us that she had decided she wanted to be around bassets again. She felt supported and understood by us and had really moved through some grief, even though we had only spoken for a short time. I explained to her that her basset girl was still around her in spiritual form. That she didn't have to prove her love by continuing to grieve. She looked at me and said, "After speaking to you, I have felt that way!" I reminded her that the degree of grieving does not equal the degree of love you have for your pet. She thanked me profusely for those words and said, "I think I'm ready to get another basset." At that moment I knew she was moving forward. Her husband vigorously thanked all of us and told us he felt he had his wife back.

An important lesson here is that she was around people who supported and understood the depth of her grief. There were no judgements, only caring support from the basset show dog community. The following year, the couple returned to the show and were ready to welcome a new basset into their lives. A show friend of ours whose wife unexpectedly made her transition, had a basset that he was ready to re-home. That basset joined their family and it is a match made in heaven.

At Faithful Friends Pet Cremation, Carolyn Hodges shares, "Families come in and just need to tell you about their pet. They NEED to tell their stories. Stories of the significance of what their pet meant to them. They need to talk and tell you the circumstances of their pet's death. We just sit there and listen. Clients will tell us that they have Rocky's ashes on the mantel or in the china cabinet, and that when they pass their pet will be buried with them." It's important to grieve and share. It's not weird or strange to want to share stories and talk about your pet. That's how we get through the pain of the physical loss. My dear friend MaryBob Straub wrote in her book, "I also know we may choose to live in those stories for a minute or a lifetime. It's a choice we make." [7]

After my experiences with my own multiple losses I knew that I needed to look inward for relief and comfort, but that inner knowledge had to be grounded in the belief that I didn't have to be in pain for a long time. That's what I recounted to the woman at the dog show. I realized that I did want to move toward a feeling of nostalgia. That feeling for me is like sadness combined with sweet memories. It is okay for me to move on from those feelings of intense and painful grief. Sometimes tears still flow when I'm feeling sad, but I'm also smiling again, like a sun shower—sun in the midst of light rain—and it actually feels good. During my times of grief this poem provides me comfort and I think it will do the same for you.

I'm Still Here

Friend, please don't mourn for me
I'm still here, though you don't see.
I'm right by your side each night and day
And with
in your heart I long to stay.
My body is gone but I'm always near.
I'm everything you feel, see or hear.
My spirit is free, but I'll never depart
As long as you keep me alive in your heart.
I'll never wander out of your sight-
I'm the brightest star on a summer night.
I'll never be beyond your reach-
I'm the warm moist sand when you're at the beach.
I'm the colorful leaves when fall comes around
And the pure white snow that blankets the ground.
I'm the beautiful flowers of which you're so fond,
The clear cool water in a quiet pond.

I'm the first bright blossom you'll see in the spring,
The first warm raindrop that April will bring.
I'm the first ray of light when
the sun starts to shine,
And you'll see that the face in the moon is mine.
When you start thinking there's no one to love you,
You can talk to me through the Spirit above you.
I'll whisper my answer through
the leaves on the trees,
And you'll feel my presence in
the soft summer breeze.
I'm the hot salty tears that flow when you weep
And the beautiful dreams that
come while you sleep.
I'm the smile you see on a baby's face.
Just look for me, friend, I'm everyplace!
—Author Unknown

By the way, it is okay if you believe differently and may not be ready to embrace these new ideas. However, I want to help bring you comfort by offering you a different possibility, a way to ease the pain, a way to move forward, and a way to get more quickly to that nostalgic feeling of sadness and sweetness at the same time. My sister, Nancy, shared that a friend said to her, "when you're going through hell, keep going!"

Do Pets Grieve Too?
About two months before my husband Paul and I got married, I went to the Suncoast Basset Hound

Rescue Waddle. This is a rescue event benefitting bassets that have ended up in shelter or foster care. I was looking across the field of bassets when I happened to see the most beautiful black basset hound with a silly hat on. I ran across the field (kind of like Bo Derek running toward Dudley Moore on the beach in the movie *10.*) I asked the owners if by any chance they had other bassets like her, and it just so happened that this basset had recently had a litter of puppies. She had an exercise-pen full of about eight puppies. One of them came right up to me, and I started petting her. They were all little beauties. I was in love and knew I HAD to have one. The breeder and I had decided to meet each other the next day so that I could see them again and maybe, hopefully, take one home. I ran home and told Paul, "I believe I found our puppy!"

Well, even though it was about two months before our wedding, and we had been saving for our honeymoon so it really wasn't a good time for a puppy, he just couldn't say no to me. I HAD to have one of those puppies! I met the owner the following day, sat in the back of her station wagon in a McDonald's parking lot, got in, and beautiful, excited, drooling, black basset hound puppies galore were all over me! The puppy who had come up to me the day before, and had picked me over several of her other siblings, became our Sophie. I was in love with this beautiful, black basset hound. There was just something about her. When I walked in the door of our home, Paul took one look at her and said, "Give me that puppy!" That was it. They were star-crossed lovers. Had my place as his fiancée been replaced by a beautiful black basset puppy? That day MY puppy became HIS puppy and they LOVED and adored each other.

Fast forward eight years. In the fall of 2014, Paul passed away. He became non-physical. It was the first time I had ever seen or experienced a dog grieving. I have had many dogs, and I have seen that not all of them appear to grieve the deaths of their housemates or owners. Even the other hounds in our household didn't appear to be affected by his death. Maybe their role was to soothe their mama. It was very apparent that Sophie was grieving Paul's death, and I really didn't know at the time what to do to ease her pain. According to Dr. Mary Burch, a certified animal behavioralist, "The signs of grieving for both dogs and people can be the same. They may lose their spark." Sophie appeared to do just that. She would lie down on the floor and just stare at the door waiting for him to come home. She would mope around the house. This went on for several days and she looked and acted miserable. I was at a loss until my sister Sally suggested that I get one of Paul's favorite hats that still had his scent on it. She suggested I put it in Sophie's crate. What a great idea! I did this, and she laid her head on it at night and covered it up with some of her bedding. It was as though she was protecting it and him. It was so poignant to see that, and I felt honored to be able to experience this level of grief with her. Giving her his hat appeared to help her move through her grieving, but I'm not sure that she ever really completely got over his death. Just a few months later I began to see her slow down and a few months after that she was diagnosed with stomach cancer. This was approximately five and a half months after Paul had passed away. Sophie was only nine years old when she passed into non-physical. I just knew at the time that she wanted to be with her daddy non-physically. It was incredibly difficult for me. But at the same time surprisingly very moving as it reminded me of those couples who have been together for 50, 60 or 70 years, and when one dies the other shortly follows.

In a similar situation, even though Moselle and my sister Sally did not live together they shared a special bond. Sally and I both believed that they were very spiritually connected. When Sally and I would talk on the phone she would always ask about Moe. When she came to visit, Moe was beside herself with joy, cooing and making special love noises that she had never made with me, my sister Nancy, Paul, Gary (my husband) or anyone else. I took some photos of the two of them together at my house, and also a precious video that my mother viewed every day. Sally suddenly passed into non-physical in the late summer of 2017. Nine months later Moe developed cancer and passed into non-physical too. I believe that even though Moe loved me very much, her bond with Sally was so strong that she wanted to join her just a few months later.

Paw Prints

🐾 Grieving is a normal emotional state that we go through after a loved one transitions to non-physical. Make sure you don't bypass this, but also don't "pitch a tent there."

🐾 The degree and length of your grieving does not equal the amount of love you have for your pet.

🐾 You don't have to be in pain for a long time.

Workbook for Chapter 3

Exercise 1 – As you begin to slightly emerge from your grieving, every morning as you wake up ask yourself, "What five things am I grateful for today?" Do this every day for several weeks.

Exercise 2 – Look for a place where you can be of service. After doing those service projects, ask yourself, "Who's life has been improved and touched today?"

Exercise 3 – Ask a friend to listen to a few joyful stories about your pet so that you are able to practice and begin to shift from sad tears to joyful tears of memories.

Death Is Nothing at All

Death is nothing at all.
It does not count.
I have only slipped away into the next room.
Nothing has happened.

Everything remains exactly as it was.
I am I, and you are you,
and the old life that we lived so fondly
together is untouched, unchanged.
Whatever we were to each other, that we are still.

Call me by the old familiar name.
Speak of me in the easy way which you always used.
Put no difference in your tone.
Wear no forced air of solemnity or sorrow.

Laugh as we always laughed at the little
jokes that we enjoyed together.
Play, smile, think of me, pray for me.
Let my name be ever the household word that it always was.
Let it be spoken without effort, without the ghost of a shadow upon it.

Life means all that it ever meant.
It is the same as it ever was.
There is absolute and unbroken continuity.
What is death but a negligible accident?

Why should I be out of mind
because I am out of sight?
I am but waiting for you, for an interval,
somewhere very near,
just around the corner.

All is well.
Nothing is hurt; nothing is lost.
One brief moment and all will be as it was before.
How we shall laugh at the trouble of
parting when we meet again!
—Henry Scott-Holland (1847 - 1918)

Chapter 4

Your Pet is a Spiritual Being Having a Canine/Feline/ Avian Experience: A New Thought Perspective

---

Let me be the voice of a good friend nudging you toward a higher truth for the sake of your peace. This book about pet "loss" was written to find its way to you and to come from a different perspective. Pierre Teilhard de Chardin, the French idealist philosopher and Jesuit priest said, "We do not believe that we are human beings having a spiritual experience, but rather that 'we are spiritual beings having a human experience.'"

SO, what if your beautiful pet was also a spiritual being having a canine/feline/avian experience? Why is it important to think of your pet's loss from a different perspective? Because New Thought philosophy teaches that life is eternal. From *the Science of Mind* by Ernest Holmes: "We accept that our physical bodies operate within a natural cycle of birth and death. However, even though we have a body, we are more than our body. We are the Life that animates our body, and that Life is infinite and immortal. As we become increasingly identified with our divine and eternal nature, our underlying fear of death dissolves and our experience of life becomes more joyous." The New Thought movement was developed in the United States in the late nineteenth century. It focused on metaphysical beliefs that included the idea that selfhood is divine (spiritual), right thinking can heal, and a higher power or "source" is a connection to the infinite. So, what if your pet just changed form from a physical manifestation to a spiritual one and they now have a spirit-pet existence?

Open yourself for a moment and suspend judgement that you've lost them and see if you can think "my pet IS here with me. I haven't REALLY lost them they are an eternal spiritual-being now! I will just have to interact/communicate/see them differently." You have a choice now. You can choose to think about your pet in terms of a physical loss or in terms of them being eternal and always with you and around you. Perhaps this is a new idea for you, and you might have to spend some time seeing if this resonates with you.

For me, it is my belief that this is the true spiritual nature of your beloved pet. You CAN choose to look at your pet's loss differently. That is one of the reasons why this book has been written and I am sharing this different way of experiencing your grief. In the 2018 movie *Mary Poppins Returns*, there is a line that says, "Nothing's gone forever, just a little out of place." I just love that little nugget of wisdom! Thinking of your pet's death differently does not mean you're not going to feel the pain, and you're not going to grieve. But once you can make the shift, it will feel less like a loss because you will connect with your pet's infinite nature more than the physical nature.

So, if you can make that jump to "they are infinite beings," then they are not really "lost." They have just changed form. Author Annie Kagan says, "When you realize that other dimensions exist, you'll never think of life, death, yourself, or the universe in the same way again." [8]

And in the same vein, Ernest Montague says in his "Rainbow Bridge Blog," "Dogs never die. They don't know how to. When you think your dog has died, it has just fallen asleep in your heart. And by the way, it is wagging its tail madly, you see, and that's why your chest hurts so much, and you cry all the time. But don't get fooled. They are not 'dead.' There's no such thing, really. They are sleeping in your heart, and they will wake up usually when you're not expecting it. It's just who they are. Dogs never die. They don't know how to." Although Mr. Montague is musing about dogs, this sentiment can be applied to any pet from hamster and fish to pig or horse!

In his book *Buddhism for Pet Lovers: Supporting our Closest Companions through Life and Death,* David Michie writes: "It's important always to remember that you don't have to believe anything. All you need is an open mind. Unless you are convinced by a different model of the death process, here, at least, is something useful that you can work with. What's more, the advantages of the practices outlined go well beyond benefiting our pets alone."

I also believe that when we and our pets become spirit, our abilities are magnified so that they don't only change from physical to spiritual form, but our pets' capabilities are more heightened and focused as well. They are letting go of the confines of their physical form and are suddenly free. This can lead to a greater ability to communicate and connect with you and you with them. They intuitively know so much about you and now there's no "body" getting in the way. They can be with you in spirit all the time now.

Why is New Thought philosophy important to understand as we learn how to grieve differently? Because what I want to share with you is there can be a quicker, easier and more comforting way to move through the grieving process if you are open to these new ideas. You may have to shift some beliefs. I didn't believe it at first until I considered the possibility of these new ideas. I had to "try them on" and see if they resonated within me. I invite you to do the same.

I learned through concepts of counseling I was exposed to while in graduate school to be a counselor, that the thoughts we think influence and create the feelings we feel. Also, that beliefs are just thoughts we think over and over again. So, when you are thinking deeply sad or angry thoughts about your pet's loss, try this: Feel those feelings and then immediately go to a better feeling thought. You may have to practice with a situation that is not so painful and have some "better feeling thoughts" ready to go. If you can do that and think about wonderful and beautiful times with your pet, then go there. But if not, you can go to any wonderful memory spent with family or friends, or the memory of a beautiful place you've visited. You may remember being together in nature, running on the beach, playing with toys, talking to your pet or just interacting with each other in a loving way.

Think a thought that brings you more peace or joy. That will assist you in lessening the suffering you are currently feeling. I feel this quote by my friend MaryBob Straub in her book *Someone Else's Shoes* is helpful for practicing going to a better feeling thought: "When thoughts of those painful moments from years (or moments) ago cross my mind, I intentionally shop the shelves of my mind for thoughts that feel better. No point in reliving what was painful."

So when you're going through the pain of grief, keep going "through it." Don't stay in that painful space, because you don't want to lose your experience of living a joyful life. When I was able to get past the shock, anger and feelings of fear/loss and remembered what I believed—my pet is a spiritual being having a canine/feline/avian/equine experience—then it suddenly occurred to me that my pets were still here with me! Now, I just had to develop a new way of communicating.

It doesn't have to be or feel weird. It can be in your mind with you just saying, *Hey, how's it going Sweetie?* Then you quiet yourself and listen for the small voice inside you. Maybe you'll even hear a response. Listen for a response—there may be a voice accompanying the spiritual experience with your pet. It's all about what you are willing to be open to. If this is beyond what resonates for you right now, that's fine … then don't go that far. Just go as far as you feel comfortable. MaryBob also writes, "I used to only feel the loss of it all and not the gratitude for the memories."

In the workbook for the previous chapter you will be beginning your mornings with the five things that you are grateful for. This will begin your journey toward healing by replacing some of your grief slowly with gratitude for the life that you shared with your pet.

Can Spirituality Be Explained Through Science?

What if all this woo-woo spiritual stuff was really based in scientific fact? I know that there are some science folks out there that may be really questioning all this. I sometimes muse about our spiritual nature and dealing with death from a scientific perspective. Like, for example, the properties of water. As we all have learned, water can be experienced in three distinct forms: ice (solid), water (liquid) and vapor (gas). When your pet is in their body they are just like ice, solid and real to our senses of touch, smell, sight, hearing and taste. But when they transition to a spiritual being after death, they become like vapor. They exist but are not easily experienced with our five senses. This is a scientific process that is provable.

Different things have different properties and they can manifest differently. Why not a being that has so much consciousness? Why would our pet be completely gone, and we be unable to experience them just because we can't see them? We cannot always see air and water or vapor and radio/light waves, and yet they exist! Modern science validates that we are made up of energy composed of molecules, protons, neutrons and electric particles that vibrate with a frequency, and that no energy dies. It just changes form. What if your dog, cat, bird, lizard, rabbit or horse is a spiritual, energetic, vibrational being having a canine/feline/avian etc.

experience and having that same vibrational experience? To me, that means when they die all they do is CHANGE FORM? Nikola Tesla, the famous scientist said, "If you want to know the universe, think in terms of energy, frequency and vibration."

Paw Prints

- "Death is only the end when you believe death is the end." – John Pete
- Your pet is a spiritual being having a (canine, feline, avian, equine etc.) experience.
- Your pet is not gone or lost; he or she has just changed form.

Workbook for Chapter 4

Exercise 1 – If these ideas of the New Thought Movement resonate with you, look in the resources and choose a book that speaks to you. Read it and see how it inspires you. Write a few thoughts that you have about a part that inspires you. (See resources for some ideas for books I like.)

Exercise 2 – Meditate on the idea that your pet is still with you in spiritual form. Journal about any signs, clues or experiences when you have felt them with you.

Exercise 3 – Help yourself deeply connect with your pet by looking at joyful and playful photographs and imagine being together and what you would be doing. Use all five senses and ask: *what would I be feeling, smelling, seeing, hearing and tasting?*

As I Sit Here Safe in Heaven

To many I am forgotten
Just a sad story from the past
but to those that love and lost me
the memories will always last

As I sit here safe in heaven
and watch you everyday
I try and let you know with signs
I never went away …

I hear you when your speaking
and watch you as you sleep
I even place my arms around you
to calm you as you weep

I see you wish the days away
as you beg to have me home
so I try and send you messages
that you are not alone

Don't feel guilty that you have a life
that was denied to me
oh, heaven is truly beautiful,
just you wait and see

Please live your life and laugh again
Enjoy yourself, be free!
Then I'll know with every breath you take
you're taking one for me...
—Hazel Birdsall Singer, 2008

Chapter 5

Now You Are Ready to Connect with Your Pet: New Steps to Healing/Signs/Interdimensional Communication

---

When your pet transitioned to non-physical, you probably felt you were no longer able to have the ease of the physical communication and the physical relationship you once had, and that is true. It will be different, and it will feel harder at first. There is a loss of that experience with your pet from the perspective of your physical senses. However, you can learn to communicate with your pet as a way of easing your grief, and it starts by focusing on the way you want to remember your pet and the wonderful times you shared. You can learn to tune in to that infinite eternal consciousness of your pet and still have a relationship with them. It will look and feel differently, and you are going to communicate with him or her differently. This phenomenon can be called "Interdimensional Communication." [9]

You will now have a different kind of relationship, and you will know that it won't be a physical one, but yours will be transformed into a spiritual relationship with your animal. You can begin this process by borrowing the belief (remembering that a belief is a thought that you think of repeatedly) that your pet is a spiritual being having a canine/feline or other experience, and then you can transform the thought that instead of your pet being gone, they have just changed form.

What if your pet's capabilities are magnified when they are in their spiritual form and they have a stronger ability to connect with you? What if, as you are practicing intentioned thought, you are also magnifying your capabilities to connect with your pet? Your pet has transformed to a spiritual form and you have the opportunity to choose to believe in the possibility that you can communicate with him or her. When they are in the physical realm, they are restricted, but now as a spiritual being they have a greater capability to connect with you, and it is likely a limitless capability.

At a recent dog show a gentleman came up to me and started telling me about his basset, Lacy. I got goosebumps when I heard him tell her story, as it reinforced how truly connected to spirit our pets can be and that they are truly spiritual beings having a canine, feline, etc. experience. He shared with me that Lacy is a pretty nonverbal basset hound except once a year on Memorial Day when he and his wife watch the Memorial Day parade on television. At some point in the parade, a musician playing a trumpet begins to play "Taps."

When Lacy hears "Taps" she throws her head back and begins to wail throughout the entire performance. Does your pet ever appear to have an emotional connection to a specific situation? What could this mean to Lacy? Could she be connecting to the spirits of fallen soldiers? I propose to stay open to the possibility. At the end of her wailing Lacy utters a little whimper that is very moving. (See both of Lacy's performances on Thepetsoulbook.com).

Earlier in the book I mentioned that my basset Moselle had a deep connection with my sister Sally. Moselle uttered sounds with Sally that she never shared with me. Moe and Sally had an emotional connection that only they shared.

How can you experience more connection with your pet? As a non-physical, eternal being, your pet is always aware of you. When you think about your pet and remember experiences you had together, that is one way that you can be aware that they are with you in the moment. When you experience places and things that you did when you were together—your walks, spending time in the dog park together, the Sunday afternoons when you sat in your living room and he or she sat there next to you, or perhaps it was your bird sitting on your shoulder or singing on her perch, or having a wonderful ride on your horse—that's how you begin to connect.

Now close your eyes and remember those feelings of being together. Get very specific and detailed. How did it look, feel, smell? What sounds did you hear? My sister, Nancy, and I were talking, and I shared with her that after Moselle and Flash passed into non-physical, I practiced walking the halls at my high school and imagined that they were walking right next to me. Very soon those images were accompanied by real feelings. Those thoughts and feelings were very soothing to me especially in the days shortly after their passing when I felt sad.

Your imagination is a very powerful tool to utilize to practice connecting with your pet in the spiritual realm. Another tool you can use is meditation, and if you are one who meditates or is willing to try it, those quiet moments can be when the non-physical metaphysical experiences may begin to happen. It may start with your feeling or sensing your pet's presence around you. When that happens, I challenge you not to immediately jump to the thoughts of "loss," but rather to comforting thoughts and feelings that they are still with you.[10]

Now that you are considering a new possibility that your pet does exist but has just transformed to a non-physical form, you can entertain the idea of interdimensional communication if you feel that you are ready for that step. A woman I work with named Myrtle shared several experiences with me about her and her son's beloved dog Chico after he made his transition to non-physical in early 2018. "I was walking down the hall and my son, Kevin, happened to have his door open and I just looked, and I saw Chico on the bed wagging his little tail and waiting for Kevin to come in. It was so peaceful. I took a second glance and he was happy and wagging his tail." I asked her if that surprised her. She went on to say, "It surprised me a little bit, but knowing that the dog was like family—he was part of the family—it didn't scare me or anything, he just let me know he was there." Myrtle and her son already had a belief that the spirit connection exists and so they were open to having and acknowledging that experience with Chico. They then felt less of a loss because they knew that he was still with them.

Another heartfelt story of pet connection came as a result of my husband having breakfast with a dear friend. Danny's beloved Chihuahua/Papillon mix, Jetta, had transitioned to non-physical about two months earlier. Danny was living by himself with Jetta and she was his world. My husband, Gary, and I would every other week get together at Danny's and meet friends to share a meal and play a friendly game of poker. Jetta would be right there with us most of the time hoping that someone would drop a wonderful morsel for her to enjoy. She was always a part of the festivities.

However, Jetta was an old girl at 14 years old and she also had some health problems. One of our friends owns a mobile vet clinic and had been assisting in her care, until one weekend she succumbed to her illness and passed away. Danny had told Gary at breakfast in a rather unremarkable way, as if it wasn't a big deal, that he had "seen" Jetta several times since her passage. Gary was overcome with emotion hearing the story and couldn't wait to tell me.

That evening was our get-together at Danny's, and at the end of the evening I asked Danny to tell me about his experiences with Jetta. He told me that when she was in the physical, she would sleep at the end of his bed every night and at 7 a.m. she would wake up and look at him. He told me that since her passing at exactly 7 a.m. on the past several mornings there she was, right at the end of his bed looking right at him! He has been so pleased with his connection but doesn't seem at all surprised. It's as though she's never left him, and she hasn't. He has had a very natural connection with her.

Creative Visualization

Now that you have embraced the idea that your pet is in spiritual form and you are open to various methods of communication and experiences, you can start trying out and practicing some of those methods. One way to soothe yourself is to use a technique called "creative visualization." Shakti Gawain wrote a book of the same name that explains how you can use the technique. You use mental imagery to create a particular outcome. I can use creative visualization to help me feel strongly that my pet's spirit is with me. "Seeing" they are with you in spirit is a powerful and soothing experience to bring you closer to them.

Creative visualization can be used during meditation. Just think about and talk to your pet, meditate and listen for the still, small voice inside that might initiate communication. You may want to contact and use an animal communicator to assist you with the process of contacting or communicating with them if that resonates with you. There is a way to soothe your feelings of "loss" by replacing them with more hopeful "they are still with me" feelings. You can feel better more quickly because you replace those feelings of loss with new feelings that feel like "hopeful nostalgia" that supports the belief they are still with you. You can even imagine (visualize) that they are walking beside you, lying at your feet in your office, etc.

Recently, I was doing my daily meditation practice before going to work. My dog Flash had been on my mind multiple times that week, and I really wasn't sure why. Months had passed since he made his transition to non-physical. All of a sudden during the meditation I felt a weight on my lap as though a dog was lying on me. Because he had been on my mind so much that week, I knew it was Flash. I was elated. I was so happy to have this encounter with him that I stayed as still as possible not wanting it to end, and it didn't until I got up from the meditation to go to work.

When we realize that we and our pets are spirit, our capabilities to connect are magnified. When our pets are spirit, not only is their form changed, but as an energetic spirit their potential is heightened and strengthened, and they are able to send and receive thoughts and communication to and from you. While in their body they are restricted to being what we have come to know as strictly physical. But an animal becoming spirit is suddenly free. Free of any restriction. Perhaps you can have a greater experience and connection with your pet because they now have a much greater ability, an expansive ability due to their spiritual nature. They intuitively know so much, they with you and you with them. On a spiritual level there is no "body" getting in the way.

Animal Communicators

Sometimes as you begin to open yourself to a new-found belief in recognizing your pet's spiritual nature, it can be helpful to get some support and assistance with your journey to communicate or to just have a deeper connection with your pet. Using a professional animal communicator can bridge that gap as you venture forward in your process. Dr. Betty Lewis, who also calls herself an Interspecies Telepathic Communicator, shares that she is an interpreter who, in communication with a person's pet, gets her messages in various forms, though typically as pictures, thoughts and feelings. She will receive information from the animal to relay to the human. She will do pre-grief counseling and regular grief counseling. Pre-grief counseling centers around the pet owners who want to know things like "when is the right time?" She then talks to the animal to get a sense of how they feel, how much they hurt and sometimes she can assist the owner in solving the medical issue that the pet may have. Her traditional grief counseling takes two forms. If there are other pets in the home, she will connect to those pets and provide support to them and help the family provide the support that they need. She will also connect to pets after they die and sometimes many years later. Dr. Lewis shares that the biggest question pet owners want to know from their pets after death is, "Are they happy?" She says the answer is 99.9 percent of the time "yes."

Dr. Lewis remembers a family who had a dog who in his prime was very territorial and energetic. He frequently guarded the perimeter of the yard and barked whenever people came to the house. The family also said he was pretty formidable. They called Dr. Lewis when he was old and "decrepit" and wanted to know if he was still happy, and if he was doing what he wanted to do in his life. He told her that he was fine and had adjusted to the point where his favorite place to lie down was right at the front door. He didn't have to get up to bark anymore and could lie there and bark at the mailman or the UPS man right from where he laid. He was happy. Later, the family reported that they learned to communicate with him themselves. So, when it was his time, he passed peacefully and the owners shared that it was a beautiful experience, mostly because they knew what he was feeling. They said too that because they had the extra time from him and with him, they didn't have the guilt that often surrounds these whole experiences.

Another experience that she had with a family was in the course of a conversation with their dog about was he ready to go. The family also asked, "What do we do to make the transition one that's comfortable for everybody?" The dog started communicating with Dr. Lewis about music and songs and after she mentioned that to the owner, he shared that he was a songwriter and that he would sing to his dog and he would "collaborate" when creating songs. She said that this was a fun experience of communication, and valuable because the owner could incorporate music into the final arrangements for his dog.

In Dr. Lewis's book *Animals Speak!* the first section is devoted to stories that animals have told her when she communicated with them. The second section of the book is a workshop for people who want to learn how to communicate with their pets and includes information and training to do so. So, if that is something that you would like to explore, I encourage you to read her book.

An Animal Communicator's View of Death from a Pet's Perspective

Over the years Dr. Lewis has communicated with pets, they have shared with her what happens after death from their perspectives. She feels that hearing this has brought comfort and peace to most with whom she's worked. She shares that when the soul or spirit passes out of the animal's body (she did see this once with her own pet whippet), it enters two concentric circles with the previous lifetime (including their loved ones) in the center of the circles. When the pets pass out of their bodies, they go into the first concentric circle and it's almost like they haven't left, as they don't have bodies or senses of time. They can be in multiple times and places. So, your loving pet can appear to you when in this realm. She says they often can appear, and if you look over your shoulder quickly you might see them. People have reported to her that they were alone in the house and yet they felt their pet (similar to my encounter with Flash on my lap when I did not see him, but I felt him). The pets also have communicated that the second concentric circle is like a "pool of souls" likened to the "Rainbow Bridge" concept. She says that there are no defined "lines" between the two circles, but that the souls can go back and forth between them like a doorway.

Maybe it is time to start being aware of your pet's and subsequently your own eternal nature. This realization may have you worrying less about death and the death process. As death is inevitable and something that happens to every physical being, maybe it is time to begin to think about transitioning from a long and sorrowful grieving process and segue to a more positive belief in the eternal nature of us all. [11]

Signs

A good way to begin the communication process, to soothe yourself and feel your pet close to you is to look for signs of them around you. I have found that even the subtle ones will give great comfort and peace and ease the feelings of missing them. I asked Myrtle if she has seen any signs since her dog Chico's transition. She shares: "My son and I were sitting in the living room, and he was in his recliner. I could see Chico walking up to him tilting his little head and wagging his tail as though to say, 'Come on, let's go to bed!'" She also shares that her daughter has had some experiences with seeing Chico. "She dreamed she saw him in a field, a beautiful field by a tree, wagging his tail like he was just waiting on us. And then she had another dream that he was in this building and he was in a cage. She got him out of the cage, and he was giving kisses, love and hugs."

Earlier I mentioned the wonderful family who had made the gut-wrenching decision to put their beloved Paco down after he was diagnosed with "rage syndrome." The day after the dog passed away, the couple with their infant son, went to a butterfly park. The woman texted me: "Went to a place called Butterfly World and a butterfly (white and brown) got on Angel's (her husband) pocket and wouldn't leave until Angel put it on a branch some 30 minutes later. I'll send you a pic. Angel said, 'Maybe it's Paco.'" Despite his disability, Paco was extremely bonded to Angel and Angel to him, so it wasn't surprising to them, or to me, that it was Angel the butterfly lit on. The butterfly wouldn't leave his pocket. I was delighted that they had this sign from their sweet dog and said, "I think Paco was definitely trying to tell you that he is still with you." Notice that it landed on his pocket (Paco). I added, "I don't believe in coincidences." I believe it was also Paco's attempt to bring them some peace and let them know he was okay.

Sometimes you will see signs in a different way that may indicate that you are in the right place at the right time. Damon LeBlanc offered this beautiful story about one of his clients at the Faithful Friends Pet Cremation Center. "A lot of families see signs. We had a sample urn displayed that had the name 'Boo-Boo' on it. I can't tell you how many people said that was their dog's name or their previous dog's name. As soon as they saw the urn, they knew it was a sign that they were at the right place for their pet."

You may be looking for a new vet, or a place to have your pet memorialized. If you find yourself seeing signs like these, it can be a comfort to move forward with them. Information that provides great clarity can be found at the backpackerverse.com blog. The blog shares four signs to look for that will indicate that your pet is reaching out to you: Feel their presence in your room. Hear them around the house. Catch a glimpse of them in your peripheral (vision). Have your thoughts change from sadness to joy from out of nowhere. Author Blair Robertson shares, "You'll know you've had a connection because you'll feel a profound sense of peace after you have completed the (communication) session." [12]

Author Margrit Coates writes: "Animal messengers travel through the dimensions of time and space to be with us. We do not have any control over this process and cannot make it happen, but when the meeting does take place, we are invited to enjoy every second of it." [13]

So how can you experience more signs from your pet? I have found that I really need to be focused and aware of everything around me and to look at things more closely. For instance, when I'm driving in my car, I'm also looking at license plates, billboards, dogs popping their heads out of car windows, street signs, business names and anything else that may be a clue that my pet is around me. From a more spiritual perspective, Whitney Hopler in her article "Signs and Messages From Animals in the Afterlife," offers: "The best way to begin is by praying; asking God to send a message from you to the departed animal indicating your desire to experience some kind of sign or receive some kind of message from that animal. Express your love wholeheartedly when you pray, since love vibrates powerful electromagnetic energy that can send signals from your soul to the animal's soul across the dimensions between Earth and heaven. Once you've prayed, open your mind and heart up to receive any communication that may come. But be sure to place your trust in God to arrange that communication at the right times and in the right ways. Be at peace that God, who loves you, will do so if it's His will."

Ms. Hopler also offers this helpful list of "signs or messages animals may send to humans from the afterlife":

- Telepathic messages of simple thoughts or feelings.
- Scents that remind you of the animal.
- Physical touch (such as feeling an animal jump up on a bed or sofa).
- Sounds (like hearing an animal's voice: barking, meowing, etc.).
- Dream messages (in which an animal usually appears visually).

- Objects related to an animal's earthly life moving (such as a pet's collar inexplicably showing up in a place where you will notice it).
- Written messages (like reading an animal's name right after thinking about that animal).
- Apparitions in visions (these are rare because they require lots of spiritual energy, but they do sometimes happen). [14]

Dr. Lewis, the animal communicator, has been told by her animal clients that some animals become guides after they pass into non-physical. One was her whippet named Halo. Halo told her that she was going to help her raise other whippets "so that it was done right," and because of that communication she had signs from Halo during the whelping of other litters. Dr. Lewis' other dog, a Great Dane named Piper, loved riding in the car. There were times when she was driving by herself and going long distances. She disliked those long trips until she realized that Piper, in non-physical form, was in the back seat which she says was very comforting to her.

If you commit to a practice of actively looking for signs around you, I believe that like me, you will experience them too. Author Sylvia Brown writes, "Be encouraged that there's a good chance you'll hear something from your beloved departed animal. Just as our loved ones who have passed over watch over us and visit us from time to time, so do our beloved pets. I have received many stories from individuals about dead pets that came back to visit. Our animals and pets that have passed over will follow us, visit us, and come around to protect us in dangerous situations." [15]

And the most encouraging words that I have read regarding signs from your beloved pet are, "Love is very powerful energy, creating its own communication network … When we love an animal a promise is made to us and it is this: *My soul will always be linked to your soul. I am with you always.*" [16]

Margrit Coates tells us, "One of the most common ways that departed animals communicate with people is by sending their signature spiritual energy to be with someone they loved on Earth. The goal is to comfort the person they loved who is grieving. When that happens, people will become aware of the animal's energy because they'll feel a presence that reminds them of that animal." [17] She goes on to quote Barry Eaton in *No Goodbyes: Life-Changing Insights from the Other Side:* "Animal spirits often come back to spend a lot of time with their former human friends, particularly those people who are on their own and very lonely. They share their energy with their human friends, and along with the person's guides and spirit helpers [like angels and saints], have their unique role to play in healing."

Kim Pardo, a colleague of mine at the high school I work at, shares an interesting story of an experience she and her husband Gerardo had while visiting a vacation home her parents had purchased in Hiawassee, Georgia. The home was originally owned by an older couple who had beloved cats. Unfortunately, the man's wife passed away from cancer and the husband moved away from the cabin. One evening, Kim and Gerardo went to bed, but she was awakened from a sound sleep. She told me that that night she had felt something nuzzle her hand. As she was still half-asleep, she reached out to pet the animal she felt, and with that Gerardo woke up and asked, "Is there a cat on the bed? I just felt one walk over me!" It turns out this was not the first time that cats had made an "appearance" at the home. After telling her mother about the surprising visit from the original owner's cat, her mother told Kim that when she and her father stayed at the house, they frequently heard a cat walking around, and up and down the stairs.

This quote from Margrit Coate's book illuminates Kim and Gerardo's experience at the cabin. "Whether or not you receive a sign or message from an animal you love in heaven, you can rest assured that anyone who is connected to you through love will always stay connected to you. Love never dies." [18] The cats wanted to be connected to the cabin of the folks they loved.

Dreams

Some pet owners have reported that they have had lucid dreams in which they have seen or even experienced their deceased pet. Jen, who writes under the Facebook account "MyBrownNewfies," shares after the passing of her beloved Newfoundland, Sherman: "Last night Sherman visited me in my dreams and it's the first time that I've seen and felt him since he died. It was amazing and I can still feel the warmth that his touch brought me... It was Sherman and he was standing on his hind legs and his arms were wrapped so securely around my upper body. I could smell his fur as my head buried into his chest and his head rested on my shoulders... I woke up from my dream not with tears but with a huge smile on my face and such a sense of comfort and relief... Sherman's visit to me last night has given me such a sense of peace."

After having shared her post she pondered, "I wonder if any of you have had the same experience with past pets?" That question elicited fourteen responses from folks eager to share their own experiences. One of them includes a dream from a pet parent about having hugged, snuggled and felt her pet's warm fur again. Another, shares being on the fence about getting another puppy until she dreamt about her dog playing with another puppy. That was the spiritual communication she needed in order to move on to another puppy to love! Most posters share that they felt their pets and smelled their fur in their dreams. Some say they dream that their pet watches over them.

In her book, *Mystical Dogs: Animals As Guides to Our Inner Life*, Jean Houston says that dogs are "holy guides to the unseen worlds." She asks: "How often do you dream of animals, have visionary experiences that involve animals, follow pathways into inner space guided by animals? Animals stretch our boundaries, prompt us to ask great questions again of ourselves and of existence." Dreams may be the gateway to communication with our departed loved ones. It will be important for you to pay attention to those special dreams and to not discount them as "only dreams."

Paw Prints

- When your pet transforms to spiritual form, they have newly magnified abilities to connect with you.
- Use tools like your imagination, dreams, meditation and creative visualization to practice connecting.
- Be open to a connection, and if needed, use a helpful facilitator such as an animal communicator to bridge the gap until you can do it on your own.

Workbook for Chapter 5

Exercise 1 – Start thinking back to any signs or experiences you may have had with your most recent pet or a previous one. Journal about those signs and experiences.

Exercise 2 – If the idea of creative visualization resonates with you, check out Shakti Gawain's book *Creative Visualization: Use the Power of Your Imagination to Create What You Want in Your Life* and do some additional exploration of the subject.

Exercise 3 – Research a local animal communicator and set up a session with him or her. If you do not feel ready to do this, go to YouTube and search and watch a few episodes.

Exercise 4 – Keep a dream journal or recording device by your bed so when you awake you can jot down or record a dream before you forget it.

I Stood by Your Bed *(Feline version)*

I stood by your bed last night,
I came to have a peep.
I could see that you were crying, you found it hard
to sleep.
I purred to you so softly as you brushed away a tear,
"it's me, I haven't left you. I'm well, I'm fine, I'm
here."
I was close to you at breakfast, I
watched you pour the tea.
You were thinking of the many times your hands
reached down to me.
I was with you at the shops today,
your arms were getting sore.
I longed to take your parcels, I wished I could do
more.
I was with you at my grave today,
you tend it with such care.
I want to reassure you that I'm not lying there.
I walked with you towards the house
as you fumbled for your key.
I gently put my paw on you, I smiled and said, "it's
me."
You looked so very tired and sank into a chair.
I tried so hard to let you know, that I was standing
there.
It's possible for me to be so near you every day.

To say to you with certainty, "I never went away."
You sat there very quietly, then
smiled, I think you knew …
In the stillness of that evening, I was very close to
you.
The day is over … I smile and watch you yawning,
and say "goodnight, God bless, I'll see you in the
morning."
And when the time is right for you
to cross the brief divide,
I'll rush across to greet you and we'll stand side by
side.
I have so many things to show you,
there is so much for you to see.
Be patient, live your journey
out … then come home to me.

—Author Unknown

Chapter 6
Filling the Void

Right after Moselle passed away the veterinarian asked me how I wanted to take care of her body. It was a difficult and painful question, but one that will likely be asked of you at the appropriate time by your veterinarian. Typically, in the past, I took my pet's body home and buried him or her in the back yard in our "doggie cemetery." But since Paul's passing, I couldn't think of anyone to dig her grave. Zach, the young man who helped me after my husband passed away, joined the Army just before Moselle and Flash's deaths.

I was looking for alternatives. I was offered the services of a local pet crematorium and discovered that it was owned by a woman with whom I had previously worked at our local high school. I think it was possible that subconsciously this may have been a sign. I really didn't especially feel like I needed to have, or keep, Moselle's ashes (because I know and believe that her spirit is still with me), but agreed to buy a package that stored her ashes in a small tasteful wooden box with her name engraved. When the pet crematorium called a few days later for me to pick up Moselle's ashes, I was extremely surprised when I opened the bag containing the box of her ashes! They had enclosed a lovely card with my Moselle's paw print on the inside and a small silk baggie tied with a satin ribbon that contained a bit of her fur. These two gifts touched me in a way I had not expected. First, when I looked at the paw print I could actually "see" her paw. It made me feel so much closer to her, as did being able to touch some of her fur. This moved me so much!

When my dear friend of many years, Susan, asked me to be with her when she put down her beloved dog Jasper at home, I was so inspired by my vet's "gift," that I brought to Susan's an ink pad, some scissors and a small silk baggie with a ribbon and was able to give her the same type of gift that I had received from the pet crematory. She was also moved. Despite her grief, she was delighted to have this remembrance of him. So, if you do not have a vet or pet crematorium, or access to some type of service that provides these keepsakes, you can ask a friend to help you. I believe that it will bring you joy and peace as it did for me and my friend as well.

There are other things that you might do to fill the void from missing the physical presence of your beloved companion. It's important to know you CAN distract yourself from the thoughts and feelings that accompany the void. One distraction strategy is to provide SERVICE to others. It may be helpful to have that service be "pet-related." I suggest volunteering at an animal shelter or a dog/cat kennel or clinic. You may want to foster an animal, volunteer with a rescue organization, or become a member of a local breed club. You could also go to a cat or dog show and offer to assist a professional or owner-handler by holding a dog or cat at ringside. Remember, this is what that couple did at the dog show, and the woman went very quickly from actively grieving to wanting to have another basset! Sometimes what is really therapeutic is to write a letter to your pet companion and share the feelings that you've been having since their passing.

I bred a litter of puppies with my bassets Winnie and Rascal. They had seven gorgeous red and white puppies, and I found wonderful homes for every one of them. I have long-standing relationships with all of their owners. In 2016, one of the bassets, Bryanna, passed away suddenly after a short and unexpected illness. Her owners, Fatima and Mateo, were devastated by her death, but at the same time wanted to fill the void with another red and white basset as much like her as possible. I really wanted to be of service to the family and cared about them very much. As a responsible, preservation breeder, I stay in touch with my families and provide support for the life of their pet, and in this case after as well. About eight months later, and while actively keeping my eyes open, I found a breeder who had a slightly older red and white basset. The breeder was thinking about placing the dog in a companion home, and I was able to get the family and the breeder together. My friends quickly fell in love with her, and now they have their new beautiful basset girl, Chanel. This family filled their void with another sweet basset hound that reminds them of their girl, Bryanna.

Sometimes finding another companion to love helps heal the void from missing your friend who has passed. This doesn't always bring peace and comfort to everyone, however, I would encourage you to consider doing it. If you do want another pet, it can sometimes be easier to consider a different breed or a different species altogether.

Another friend's husband was very resistant to getting another dog after their beloved schnauzer had passed away. He felt that he wasn't ready, and he still felt he was in the depths of his grieving. His wife was very ready and desperately wanted another dog. She met me at a dog show and we went to visit the rings where the schnauzer exhibitors were showing. She was hoping to meet up with a past breeder of one of her dogs. Although she didn't meet up with her former breeder, she did meet and begin talking to a breeder who had a retired show dog she was hoping to place in a companion pet home. A few months passed before my friend actually brought her home after talking it over with her husband. He was still guarded but willing to be open. When my friend brought the new schnauzer home, her husband fell hopelessly in love with her and was able to move more quickly through his grieving process. It can be very therapeutic to have a pet companion and therefore very helpful to have one (or more) that will assist you in moving through your grief and filling that void left by the passing of the other.

I found that having my other pets around me after the passing of Moselle and Flash was ultimately one of the most helpful things to move me through my grieving process. I was able to hug and love on my other guys, and that helped ease my feelings of grief. Author Dr. Nick Trout drives this point home: "It may be a cat, a bird, a ferret, or a guinea pig, but the chances are high that when someone close to you dies, a pet will be there to pick up the slack. Pets devour the loneliness. They give us purpose, responsibility, a reason for getting up in the morning, and a reason to look to the future. They ground us, help us escape the grief, make us laugh, and take full advantage of our weakness by exploiting our furniture, our beds, and our refrigerator. We wouldn't have it any other way. Pets are our seat belts on the emotional roller coaster of life—they can be trusted, they keep us safe, and they sure do smooth out the ride." [19]

I asked my colleague Myrtle what was the most encouraging, loving and helpful thing that someone has said when she is grieving the loss of a pet. She replied that when I comforted her after hearing of her dog's transition and said, "he's not with you physically, but he's still with you spiritually. The soul of your dog is still with you." I also asked her what she and her son had done to help soothe themselves during this difficult time? She explained, "We've talked about him and talked about his burial plans." Other ways to fill the void might include going to a support group, getting a temporary or permanent tattoo of your pet, or having an artist paint or draw a portrait of your pet.

Should You Seek "Closure?"

At the time of your pet's death and during your grieving period, many people, including some therapists and grief counselors, talk about the concept of getting closure around the transition. Sometimes you will hear from very well-meaning and well-intentioned folks that you need to just "let go," "have closure" or "move on." However, since we are (and your pet is) eternal, why would we need or want closure? Do you believe that all energy and consciousness are really always in motion and in existence? Why would we have to close the door on a relationship, when the big door of communication and connection is wide open? And would you want to deliberately keep from thinking of your pet when that will be the very thing that keeps the connection open? [20]

I do believe that getting closure around the grieving process is helpful, but I don't believe that closure around your relationship is necessary, that is if you believe that the eternal and spiritual nature of your pet is still with you and around you. It's comforting to know that your loved one still exists in another form and that there is a way to tap into their very essence. Author Nora McInerny says in her TED Talk on not moving on after the experience of multiple family deaths, "I haven't moved on, and I hate that phrase so much, and I understand why other people do, because what it says is, Aaron's (her husband) life and death and love are just moments that I can leave behind me and that I probably should—so I've not moved on FROM Aaron, I've moved forward WITH HIM."

I believe that we can say the same thing about our pets. We are forever changed and better for having shared our lives with them, and when we receive a new pet into our home, we love that pet having known and loved our former beloved pet. We are moving forward "with them." Nora also shares that "we don't look at the people around us experiencing life's joys and wonders and tell them to 'move on,' do we? We need each other to remember, to help each other remember, that grief is this multitasking emotion. That you will be sad, and happy. You'll be grieving and able to love in the same year, or week, the same breath." She then says, "But yes, absolutely, they're (the grieving person) going to move forward. But that doesn't mean they've moved on." I found Nora's words comforting when I was grieving as I began to believe that I could feel all these emotions at the same time.

Rituals and Altars

During this time of grieving and healing it can be helpful to begin some rituals that will help you feel a deeper sense of connection with your pet, but also help bring some closure to your transition and grieving process. It may be helpful to have a pet funeral, celebration of life or ceremony. These have been done for many years in many civilizations. Your ceremony can be as simple or as elaborate as you would like, and you can bring in a spiritual or religious tone or not. You will find that planning and carrying out your ceremony can be very therapeutic and bring you to feeling closer to your pet. You may say a few words, read a poem, sing or play a special song, release balloons, plant a tree or flowers, bury your beloved friend in a special place with a special marker that you can purchase or create, light candles, release lanterns or any ritual that feels meaningful to you.

Popular now are pet crematoriums and funeral homes that specialize in commemorating your pet's passage into non-physical. If you decide to have your pet cremated, there are some lovely jewelry pieces in which you can have your pet's ashes encased. One person took her cat's collar with his name on it and placed it around a planter and planted a special arrangement in it. She went on to display it on her desk at work and looked at it every day. Watering the plant brought her peace and a feeling of closeness to him.

Remember the story of the songwriter who after speaking to the animal communicator discovered the songs that his pet loved and planned to incorporate them into their pet funeral planning? If you are doing your ritual with family and friends who knew your pet, it can be very cathartic to share happy memories, stories and times together. When my husband Paul and I established our dog cemetery in the back yard, he built a little bench, put an umbrella, a few stones and an urn with flowers around the area. It was a peaceful and beautiful space for me to quiet myself, meditate and think about the memories of our pets.

Patti Wigington suggests a pet farewell ritual after your pet passes away in which you gather salt, stones, incense and water and say the following prayer:

Pass the stones over the salt, and say:

<Pet's name>, with the energies of Earth, I am with you in spirit. Your memory will always remain with me.

Pass the stones over the incense, and say:

<Pet's name>, with the energies of Air, I am with you in spirit. Your memory will always remain with me.

Pass the stones over the candle, and say:

<Pet's name>, with the energies of Fire, I am with you in spirit. Your memory will always remain with me.

Pass the stones over the water, and say:

<Pet's name>, with the energies of Water, I am with you in spirit. Your memory will always remain with me. [21]

When my first basset Sophie passed into non-physical, I could not come back to school that day after being at the vet and experiencing her passing. I called my friend and colleague Tammy at school and asked her to bring to her office my student, friend and neighbor Zach, and ask him if he would be willing to dig a grave for Sophie. Now, he had done many dog-related chores and jobs for me over the past eight months after my husband had passed away, but this was personal and special. However, at only 17 I wasn't really sure he was emotionally ready for this.

Tammy sent for Zach and when he got to her office, she told him about Sophie's passing. During their conversation Tammy later shared that he asked her, "How am I going to comfort Mrs. Moore?" He appeared concerned that he might not have the right words to say. She told him to just "be there for her." Later that afternoon, right after school, he came down to my house. Slowly and with such care and patience, he dug her grave. I have never seen a more perfect job. It was a spiritual experience watching him dig my little girl's grave and final resting place for her physical form.

Paul's mother had asked earlier if she could come and bring some of Paul's ashes to the grave site to sprinkle over Sophie's grave. I thought that it was a beautiful idea signifying the closeness they shared, two bodies intertwined. Zach, Mom Moore and I stood over the grave as we laid her body to rest, cried, hugged and said a few words. Mom Moore then sprinkled some of Paul's ashes in the grave. It was deeply moving. Through this poignant and moving tribute we all grew closer and shared something we'll all never forget. I felt much closer to

Sophie, Zach and Mom Moore that day, and I know that the experience was meaningful to them as well.

Rituals can be created in any form. You can create a collage or shadowbox of photos and special mementos, or a compilation video to be shared and viewed at the celebration and that can be revisited for years to come. Another popular way to acknowledge your pet's passing is to create an altar. It can be as simple or elaborate as you want to make it, and you can find many ideas on sites such as Pinterest. An example of creating a simple altar is to take a shadow or cigar box and decorate it with paw prints of decoupage and place mementos such as your pet's collar (if they had one), tags, favorite small toy, photo, or any special item that reminds you of them when they were in physical form. You could also purchase one of those electronic picture frames to be included in the altar that can scroll through your favorite photos. There are many internet sites that have meaningful items that you can purchase. Also, if you have children, have them create drawings or paintings for your altar. Kids come up with some of the most creative things. If you have a few special blankets your pet used, creating a mini-quilt can be a wonderful memorial item for an altar or it can be used as a healing project.

Some additional examples of rituals that you can try, include:

- Donating to a favorite pet-related organization

- Writing an obituary and posting it on an online memorial from a local newspaper
- Adding urns and cremation jewelry
- Commissioning a special portrait of your pet by a local artist
- Getting a temporary or permanent tattoo of your pet

Another way to connect and ritualize your pet's passing is to observe National Pet Memorial Day. It is commemorated on the second Sunday in September and has been observed for the past 40 years. Owners can celebrate and honor their loved one's each year on this special day by reflecting on their memories of them. You can also share memories and photos of your transitioned pet on social media using the hashtag #nationalpetmemorialday.

Paw Prints

- Discover a meaningful way to memorialize your pet that will help you remember and connect with joy.
- You don't have to move ON, but definitely move FORWARD and THROUGH your grief.
- Be mindful that you are creating powerful memories surrounding your pet's passing with the human loved ones in your life, sometimes bringing you closer.

Workbook for Chapter 6

Exercise 1 – Start exploring pet memorial rituals that might be meaningful to you. Choose one and begin to work on bringing it to life.

Exercise 2 – Explore charitable and service work projects in your community and volunteer for one that resonates with you. You may really benefit from choosing one that is pet-related.

Exercise 3 – Build a pet memorial altar. Be creative.

Life and Death are but an illusion.
Happy and Sad are just a state of mind.
Love and Compassion alleviates the suffering
Of All sentient Beings—those who have been
our Mothers and our Fathers.
To recognize the interconnectedness of all beings
Is to know peace!
                    —a Buddhist homage

Chapter 7

What Do You Do If a Person You Love Has a Beloved Pet That Has Died?

If you are reading this book and are planning to offer it as a gift to a beloved person in your life who has experienced the death of their pet, you may also be seeking guidance as to what to say or do next. By gifting this book to them you have taken that first important step of acknowledging their connection with their loved one and are helping to seek a way to soothe their heartbreak.

As a counselor, what I typically hear from students, friends and clients is that they just want to be heard and to talk about their pet. It is important to realize that you will not make your friend sadder by asking about how they are feeling. They are already always thinking about it and you won't remind them that their pet has died. Although they may cry while sharing, expressing their emotions is an important part of the healing process and you are giving them a great gift to be able to express it with a safe person. However, it is important that what you say and ask is helpful and appropriate. Sometimes, even the most well-intentioned person may say things to a grieving person that aren't helpful. More recently, people are more open to recognizing that the grief people experience around their pet's death is just as deep and painful as any experience with human death as sometimes that pet is their significant other or has been the only creature from which they have experienced unconditional love.

Sometimes they grew up with their pet or they are a single person whose whole life revolves around it. When my husband died and I was alone in the house, it was my beloved basset hounds that soothed me with their love and attention. Taking care of them provided me with much needed distraction from my feelings of grief around my husband's death. When a person is alone but has a pet, they really aren't alone at all and that relationship can become their whole world.

Below is a series of helpful talking points that I discovered on the Pet Loss Support Page (see resources) that will help give you the compassionate words to comfort that friend in need.

Please do not say: It's not like you lost a child.	**Instead say**: I know that you cared very much for (insert pet's name).
Please do not say: Oh well it was only a cat (or dog, bird, horse, hamster, fish etc.).	**Instead say**: You must miss (insert pet's name) very much. He/she was a part of the family.
Please do not say: So when are you getting another pet?	**Instead say**: What can I do to help?
Please do not say: He/she is better off now. It's for the best.	**Instead say**: You did everything you could.
Please do not say: You'll feel better soon.	**Instead say**: He/she was so lucky to have you.
Please do not say: I know exactly how you feel.	**Instead say**: Tell me more about (pet's name).
Please do not say: You must feel awful.	**Instead say**: He/she couldn't have had a better owner.
Please do not say: Get over it.	**Instead say**: I'm so sorry.
Please do not say: Don't cry.	**Instead say**: Why don't you share with me how you're feeling.
Please do not say: It's a good thing that you have other animals.	**Instead say**: It's totally understandable that you are grieving right now.

By using more comforting and appropriate words, you will help your friend and loved one feel understood and supported and help them soothe the feelings of grief needed for their healing.

In the internet age we are more frequently wanting to help others virtually and we express our condolences online even to strangers. If you are reading this book, you have an intimate connection with the love we share between ourselves and our beloved pets. You want to reach out, but what do you say? I became aware that most well-intentioned people will often say some form of, "I'm sorry for your loss" and unwittingly reinforce the "loss" of their deceased pet. At the beginning, I also struggled with finding the right words to express my condolences for their experience and feelings of grief. I wanted to say it in a way that emphasized my support for their healing. I will typically post, "I am sending you light and love for your comfort and healing during this difficult time." I also found a wonderful article written by Blake Flannery entitled, "Pet Sympathy Messages: Condolences for Loss of Dogs, Cats and Other Pets." A couple of suggestions written by Mr. Flannery, or the one I created above, will help convey the right balance of your support and compassion. They are:

- "May you be comforted by the peace of knowing that you provided a loving home to your awesome pet for several years."
- "Most people treat their pets like friends and family, but I think you treated yours even better."

- "There's definitely something special between dogs (or any pet) and their owners, and it's called unconditional love."
- "You had one of the coolest dogs (or any pet) I have ever had the pleasure of being around."
- "I know that your (pet's name) can never be replaced. Great dogs (or cats, horses, rabbits, birds, etc.) like yours are rare."

Sometimes you may also want to post a comforting quote to someone or add one to a card or gift (like this book). Here are some additional suggestions taken from Mr. Flannery's article:

- "Until one has loved an animal, a part of one's soul remains unawakened." —Anatole France
- "Dogs are not our whole life, but they make our lives whole."
  — Roger Caras
- "My little dog–a heartbeat at my feet."
  — Edith Wharton
- "The poor dog, in life the firmest friend, the first to welcome, foremost to defend."
  — Lord Byron
- "Dogs do speak, but only to those who know how to listen."
  — Orhan Pamuk
- "Our perfect companions never have fewer than four feet."
  — Colette [22]

So many of these quotes and messages are "dog"-centered, but if you look at them carefully, they all can be revised to reflect any beloved pet. They can add a beautiful message of joy and comfort. Also, do not be afraid to write an original quote or heartfelt message to your friend or loved one like the one that I shared.

Paw Prints

- It is important to find the right words to convey your support and understanding for your friend or loved one who has just experienced their pet's death.
- Do not be afraid to let your friend or loved one share experiences or thoughts about their pet.
- It's okay for your friend or loved one to cry, it supports their healing process.

Workbook for Chapter 7

Exercise 1 – Visit some pet-related Facebook sites and practice appropriately responding to those folks who have recently experienced the death of their pet. This will give you an experience of providing service to others and help you move through your own healing process.

Exercise 2 – If you are supporting a friend or loved one who has just had a pet transition to non-physical, practice active listening. Active listening includes showing genuine concern, paraphrasing to show you understand the feelings of your friend, providing nonverbal cues which show understanding such as nodding, maintaining eye contact and leaning forward. You can also use responses such as "I see," "I know," "Sure," "Thank you," or "I understand."

We Are All One

Within you lies the Sun, the Moon, the sky and all the wonders of this Universe. The intelligence that created these wonders is the same force that created you. All things around you come from the same source. We are all one. Every being on this earth, every object on this Earth has a soul. All souls flow into one, this is the Soul of the universe. You see, when you nourish your own mind and your own spirit, you are really feeding the Soul of the Universe. When you improve yourself, you are improving the lives of all those around you. And when you have the courage to advance confidently in the direction of your dreams, you begin to draw upon the power of the Universe. Remember, life gives you what you ask for it. It is always listening.

—Robin S. Sharma

Chapter 8
Pet Loss and Connection: A Global and Spiritual Perspective

All over the world people from different cultures and religions cope with the transition of their pets into non-physical in many ways. Because of ethnic differences they may view death and react to the death process differently, but those views can also be surprisingly similar. I believe that as we see other cultures revere their pets and companions as much as we do in the West, especially from times past, it can give us support and reinforce that our feelings are real and meaningful. Matt Weiser writes of the Central Valley Indian Tribe of California people who buried their dog's side by side with them. Their companions were family pets and they did not have pet cemeteries. They were buried with their owners. [23]

David Michie writes about the Tibetan Buddhist practice of being with your pet during the death process. He feels that "We should be trying to put aside our own feelings of grief and loss and do all we can to help them have a painless, peaceful and even positive death experience." He also explains that the Buddhist belief is that immediately after a pet's death there is an intermediate or "bardo" state that may last from a few days to several weeks and that it is wiser to "focus on the well-being of our pet as opposed to our own sense of loss." Mr. Michie adds, "Much of the unhappiness surrounding death arises from our quite natural sense of loss. But we do have a choice. By focusing on our loved one's conscious-ness as it moves from one realm of experience to the next, we are able to cope with the death of our pet with greater compassion and equanimity." [24] This reinforces the idea introduced in Chapter 4 suggest-ing that you shift your focus to the spiritual nature of your pet instead of the physical.

In a work by George Catlin published in 1856 he describes that "Indian men hunted with their dogs, the women used them to assist in their physical labors, and children played with them. Dogs weren't just pets, but members of the tribe and were known and loved by tribe people as one loves a co-worker, a friend or a family member. It was believed that dogs could see the dead and portend the future." The bond between the Indian and his or her dog was deep and meaningful. In fact, an Indian legend popular in memes regarding the human death transition says, "When a human being dies there is a bridge they must cross to enter into heaven. At the head of the bridge waits every animal that human encountered in their lifetime."

In the book, *My Pig Amarillo*, author Satomi Ichikawa, reveals the sense of loss that a young Guatemalan boy feels for his pet pig. To help soothe him, his grandfather says they can send a message with a kite on All Saints' Day. The young boy works hard on his kite, sending it into the sky at the cemetery. Then, over a mountain appears an enormous cloud. It's in the shape of a pig, and to the boy, it seems his pet is smiling down at him. The boy sees a sign from his pet! [25] The boy's grandfather is trying to show his grandson the deep connection that we have with our pet after their death, and if we reach out and attempt to establish contact using any method including a kite, if we believe, we can have that connection.

In the Hindu religion it's been said that dogs guard the entrance of heaven and hell. It was also reported in *The Times of India*, "When a dog or cat or any animal for that matter dies it goes straight to Yamaloka (place of peace) so Yamadev (God of death) can allocate that soul a new body in its next birth." *The Times* goes on to say, "According to Hinduism, spiritually there is no distinction between human beings and other life forms. All life forms, including plants and animals, are manifestations of God as limited beings (jivas) and possess souls." *The Times* provides the following guidance: "If your animal is about to leave their body, try to chant the Maha Mantra or any mantra that you feel comfortable with ... Try to make your pet drink some Ganga water, eat a little Prashad, and try to make sure it's comfortable ... When your pet soul has left its body this is called death and now you need to still put a few drops of Ganga water in its mouth and then place a few Tulsi Twigs into its mouth ... This ensures your animal will get a very nice higher birth in its next life."

Phylameana lila Desy writes in an article called, "Spirit Communication with Deceased Pets," that the character George says, "It was a Passover Seder and the time had come to open the door to allow the prophet Elijah to enter, should he choose to do so. My stepdaughter opened the door and in walked our Elijah. (In life, he had been a stray that they welcomed into their home), and of course he had to have that name. About five years old at that time, he lived with us for the next 15 years until a couple of months ago. He and I were joined at the hip my wife said. I miss him so very much. I did see his spirit once stretching on the front of a living room chair. I miss him beyond belief." [26] So not only did George and his family experience a visitation by their beloved Elijah, but he was brought forward by summoning the prophet by the same name.

In Japan, Chisato Tanaka wrote about a unique business named Pet Loss Café that invites people who have experienced the death of their pets to come to a safe and supportive place to grieve, free of ridicule from people who do not understand the level of grief and connection we have with our pets. The staff is compassion-trained and also available to talk. As the customer orders a beverage, they also complete a form that shares information about their departed pet. They are asked if they want to talk or prefer to be left alone. Also, Japan's largest producer of accessories for pet altars has a café/gift shop at their home office where customers may buy altars and accessories. While they are sipping a beverage and shopping, they are encouraged to talk about their pet with a trained staff. Megumi Kawasaki, a counselor specializing in folks dealing with the passing of their pet acknowledges that "most of her clients were women in their 40s and 50s who cared for their pets as a member of their family. In serious cases, some cannot leave their house for a year and consider ending their lives. (Losing pets) really is nothing different from losing your (human) loved ones, and sometimes it can be even worse for cat or dog owners who must face the sudden lack of a partner that used to stick with them all the time." [27]

The Bible also weighs in on animals and the afterlife. In Isaiah 11:6–8 and 65:25, the prophet lists numerous animals while describing the eternal kingdom of God. In Romans 8:18–25, God's promises portray a world to come in which animals will know the peace they too have longed for. An article by Adam Epstein states that Pope Francis said that "all pets go to heaven" and Pope John Paul II said in 1990 that "animals have souls." Mormons also believe that animals go to heaven. They believe that we may be able to communicate with our pets in the afterlife. [28] In Krista Cook's, "What Mormons Believe About Pets in the Afterlife," she writes that Mormon founder Joseph Smith taught that he had "heard the words of the beasts giving glory to God and understood them." [29] The Bible also says that the sores of Lazarus were licked by dogs which then quickened the healing process. [30]

Paw Prints

🐾 Knowing that people from other cultures also revere their pets supports and reinforces our own feelings of connection.

🐾 Some cultures believe that we can have a deep connection with our pets after their deaths.

🐾 Many religious texts, including the Bible, have been interpreted to say that pets have souls.

Workbook for Chapter 8

Exercise 1 – Make an appointment with your religious or spiritual leader for support.

Exercise 2 – If you are not affiliated with a particular faith or spiritual belief system, research a book that you might connect to on the subject.

Exercise 3 – Research you own religion to discover its views on pets and the afterlife. Come to your own conclusions regarding your own faith-based philosophy.

Afterword

The Difference Between "Animal Rights" and "Animal Welfare"

There is a great difference between identifying as an animal welfare activist and an animal rights activist. As a pet lover, you may want to explore these two schools of thought and I encourage you to do your research and come to your own conclusions. Organizations such as PETA and The Humane Society of the United States are not who you might think they are, and I was surprised with what their ultimate goals are. Please check out my essay titled, "Things to Ponder and Consider as a Loving Pet Owner: Pet Owner or Pet Parent?" at my websites: Thepetsoulbook.com or Juliemooreauthor.com.

Pet Soul Resources

Paws for Thought: A Pet Counselor's Reflections

Whenever you are grieving it is perfectly natural to feel sadness. It is a normal human emotion that will assist you in your healing process. In the previous pages, my hope is that you found sources of support that resonate with you and guide you to a place of peace. However, if you find yourself going from sadness to depression, feeling a deep sense of hopelessness or having thoughts of suicide, it is important to seek the help and advice of a professional immediately. One who specializes and supports people who have experienced the death of their pet would be ideal.

You may also find benefit and comfort from attending a pet support group at your local pet crematorium, local church, or community center, or you can ask your vet to provide you with a referral to a helping professional. If you feel you need support, I encourage you to find it, and reach out for it! Do not wait. Tell someone! Included in this chapter are some resources to help you with your healing process and/or developing communication with your pet.

In my research, I have discovered that there are many online support resources. Make sure when you are grieving, you're not turning to unhealthy things that can further complicate your pain and inhibit your ability to move through your grief and connect with the soul of your pet. Instead of healthy and truly helpful supports, some can become addictive behaviors such as using alcohol, food, etc. to help ease pain. When you are feeling particularly sad, try one of these suggestions on this to do list to distract you from feelings of loss. The suggestions are offered to ease your discomfort.

Pet Soul "To Do" List
Jot down a few notes about how you felt regarding your activity and check off when completed.

	NOTES	COMPLETED
Find your favorite songs and sing or dance to them		

Take a hike		
Walk at the local high school track		
Ride your bicycle		
Find some old "I Love Lucy" Episodes (or favorite comedies) to binge watch.		
Begin a mindfulness meditation practice (There are several wonderful apps out there that are free to use to start your journey. My personal favorite is "Insight Timer.")		
Do some mindful deep breathing exercises		
Begin a yoga practice or just take a class		
Invest in a gym membership and work out with others (Sometimes you can qualify for a free membership!)		
Contribute to a research organization looking for a cure to the disease that contributed to your pet's death		
Go to a counselor or therapist		

Websites

- **The Petsoulbook.com – This book's official website**
- The Association for Pet Loss and Bereavement: aplb.org
- Pet-loss.net
- Thelapoflove.com
- Funeralwise.com
- Centerforpetlossgrief.com
- Critters.com
- Justovertherainbowbridge.com
- Petloss.com
- Tribute.perfectmemorials.com
- Pethelpful.com

Songs

Sometimes listening to a special song will help you tap into feelings that can provide support and understanding. Listening to music can bring on extreme feelings of sadness, so make sure you're ready or have support nearby. These songs can remind you that you aren't alone with your feelings. Some of my personal favorites I found while researching using YouTube are:

Song	Artist/Notes
"I Will Always Be with You"	by Sheena Easton and Jesse Corti. From the movie: *All Dogs Go to Heaven*. This song is a tribute to the human/dog bond.

"I'll See You Again"	by WestLife. Lyrics include: "I'll see you again … you never really left … I feel you walk beside me, I know I'll see you again … No, this is not goodbye."
"Come to Me"	by Hiroshima. Lyrics include: "Come to me … Can you see … Love is never gone … Believe in me … I'll be there … No matter where … You can always count on me … you will see."
"My Old Dog"	by Ronnie Buss. This song is the story of a man who has just put his dog to sleep. Lyrics include: "And though his body failed, His spirit still prevailed, And it will live on … Making me strong cause my old dog went to sleep today. And as time goes by, I still break down and cry. But it ain't for long, I just sing this song And my old dog is with me today. Someday when it's right, our souls will reunite, and we will live on forever as one … cause my old dog sent me peace today!"

Books

Below is a list of books that you may find interesting to help you continue your journey of expansive thought. Some have been mentioned in this book. Some are just special to me.

Someone Else's Shoes: Walking the Muddy Path Toward Personal Sovereignty	MaryBob Straub (2019). DreamSculpt Books and Media, an imprint of Waterside Productions.
Creative Visualization: Use the Power of Your Imagination to Create What You Want in Your Life	Shakti Gawain (2016). New World Library; 40th Anniversary Edition.
Animals Speak!	Betty Lewis, RVT, Dr. A.N. (2001). Author House (available at Authorhouse.com).
Sculptor in the Sky	Teal Swan (2011). Author House.
On Death & Dying: What the Dying Have to Teach Doctors, Nurses, Clergy & Their Own Families	Elizabeth Kubler-Ross (2014). Scribner Publishing.
The Power of Awareness	Neville Goddard (1952). Penguin Group.
The Power of Decision: A Step-By-Step Program to Overcome Indecision and Live Without Failure Forever	Raymond Charles Barker (2011). Tarcher Perigee.
The Untethered Soul: A Journey Beyond Yourself	Michael A. Singer (2007). New Harbinger Publications/ Noetic Books.

Discover The Power Within You: A Guide to the Unexplored Depths Within	Eric Butterworth (2008). Harper One; Anniversary Edition
A New Earth: Awakening to Your Life's Purpose	Eckhart Tolle (2008). Penguin.
The Power of Now: A Guide to Spiritual Enlightenment	Eckhart Tolle (2004) New World Library.
The Four Agreements: A Practical Guide to Personal Freedom (A Toltec Wisdom Book)	Don Miguel Ruiz (1997). Amber-Allen Publishing.
Home With God: In A Life That Never Ends	Neale Donald Walsch (2006). Atria Books.

Podcasts

There are some podcasts that speak from various perspectives on the death of a pet. I am hopeful that while reading this book you have grown to see beyond the physical loss to a continuing relationship with your pet. I do see value in these methods of support. It's important for you to know that these podcasts are out there, and that you know you are not alone with your grieving and that you're not crazy for feeling the way you do.

"Pet Life Radio"	Has many different podcasts regarding pets in general.
"Alive Again: Animal Reincarnation"	Nine Lives with Dr. Kat – Episode 49.

Continue

"You Are Not Crazy"	Pet loss grief.
"Paranormal Pets"	Episode 70: Coping with Pet Challenges, Illnesses and End-of-Life Issues.
"Healing Pet Loss"	Hosted by Marianne Soucy.
"The Bond"	Finding Solace After the Loss of a Pet – Glass beads with cremation ashes.
"Dog Cast Radio"	Episode 173: Pet Loss and End-of-Life.
"Moving On"	Grieving the loss of a pet. Short three-minute podcast with someone sharing their experience.
"Nobody Told Me!"	Jan Black/Laura Owens – Guest, Guy Winch on how terribly painful the loss of a pet is; Ted Talk available.

Altar and Ritual Internet Sites

Custompeturns.com

Etsy.com › market › pet altars

Google: "How to create an altar for your pet"

GoodTherapy.org. Creating Shrines and Altars for Healing from Grief. Karla Helbert, MS, LPC. (This article shares information on creating an altar for a human, but most of the suggestions can be used for your pet too.)

Miscellaneous

Abraham material (website, books, CD's Mp3's, etc.).
Abraham-Hicks Publications; abraham-hicks.com

Other important steps you may want to consider:

Pet Trusts. It's important to do some end-of-life planning for yourself as it impacts your pets. I set up a trust with specific instructions for my executor. Suncoast Basset Hound Rescue will assist with finding new forever homes for my pets. Funds will be provided for those new families and the Suncoast Rescue Organization. I know my family is well-meaning, yet they may not have the expertise or desire to take on the difficult challenge of finding new homes for my pets upon my death. For most of us, especially with the advent of social media, there isn't a week that goes by when we aren't asked to help re-home a pet. I want to be sure that if I enter hospice or upon my death, my family can be proactive. My great desire is to ensure my beloved pets' lives will continue to be filled with love. I am sure that you feel the same way!

Pet Cremation.
You may seek out the services of a pet cremation business. The one I mention is in my hometown, and it will give you an idea of what you can expect.
Faithful Friends Pet Cremation, Zephyrhills, Florida—Carolyn Hodges, Damon and Rachel

LeBlanc, owners. Their service is for the end-of-life care for pets and other animals (dogs, cats, fish, as well as kangaroos, lions and tigers). They are there with end-of-life services to assist in memorializing your animal/pet/significant other and they're in business to help families get through the death of their pet with whatever meaning that has for them. They also offer burial services, urns, jewelry and other mementos, as well as pets' paw prints and fur clippings. They don't have a pet cemetery but can offer caskets, grave markers and shrines. Their goal is to help folks through the difficult experience and to help families find closure to their loved one's death experience. They strive to be helpful in simplifying their client's experience, and one that is something that will support them. They want to support the honoring of their pet. One example is they are open to having the family put their pet in the cremation chamber and stay for the cremation. One client said to Damon, "If the roles were reversed, they would be there for me." Damon shared there was a family that requested he release a little smoke from the cremation machine so they could see their pet's essence and spirit released into the atmosphere. Damon and the crew agreed, and the family was very appreciative.

Water Cremation

A burial or traditional cremation will not be a fit for every pet owner, so you may want to explore water cremation. Their technology and process called "Aquamation" is claimed to be environmentally safe. There is a company in Florida by the name of "Natures Pet Loss," for example. If you are interested in more information, you can explore their website at: NaturesPetLoss.com or Google "pet water cremation" for a company that provides this service closer to you.

Short Stories to Inspire and *Soothe*

The Fourth Day
by Martin Scot Kosins

If you ever love an animal, there are three days in your life you will always remember...

The first is a day, blessed with happiness, when you bring home your young new friend. You may have spent weeks deciding on a breed. You may have asked numerous opinions of many vets or done long research in finding a breeder. Or, perhaps in a fleeting moment, you may have just chosen that silly looking mutt in a shelter simply because something in its eyes reached your heart.

But when you bring that chosen pet home, and watch it explore, and claim its special place in your hall or front room, and when you feel it brush against you for the first time, it instills a feeling of pure love you will carry with you through the many years to come.

The second day will occur eight or nine or ten years later. It will be a day like any other. Routine and unexceptional. But, for a surprising instant, you will look at your longtime friend and see age where you once saw youth. You will see slow deliberate steps where you once saw energy. And you will see sleep when you once saw activity. So, you will begin to adjust your friend's diet, and you may add a pill or two to her food. And you may feel a growing fear deep within yourself, which bodes of a coming emptiness. And you will feel this uneasy feeling, on and off, until the third day finally arrives.

And on this day, if your friend and God have not decided for you, then you will be faced with deciding on your own on behalf of your lifelong friend, and with the guidance of your own deepest Spirit. But whichever way your friend eventually leaves you, you will feel as lone as a single star in the dark night.

If you are wise, you will let the tears flow as freely and as often as they must. And if you are typical, you will find that not many in your circle of family or friends will be able to understand your grief, or comfort you.

But if you are true to the love of the pet you cherished through the many joy-filled years, you may find that a soul, a bit smaller in size than your own, seems to walk with you, at times, during the lonely days to come.

And at moments when you least expect anything out of the ordinary to happen, you may feel something brush against your leg, very, very lightly.

And looking down at the place where your dear, perhaps dearest, friend used to lay, you will remember those three significant days. The memory will most likely be painful and leave an ache in your heart. As time passes the ache will come and go as if it has a life of its own.

You will both reject it and embrace it, and it may confuse you. If you reject it, it will depress you. If you embrace it, it will deepen you. Either way, it will still be an ache.

But there will be, I assure you, a fourth day when along with the memory of your pet, and piercing through the heaviness in your heart, there will come a realization that belongs only to you. It will be as unique and strong as our relationship with each animal we have loved and lost. This realization takes the form of a Living Love, like the heavenly scent of a rose that remains after the petals have wilted. This Love will remain and grow and be there for us to remember. It is a love we have earned. It is the legacy our pets leave us when they go. And it is a gift we may keep with us as long as we live. It is a Love which is ours alone. And until we ourselves leave, perhaps to join our Beloved Pets, it is a Love we will always possess.

Old Dogs Don't Die
by Leigh Hester

Old dogs don't die; they can't. They've merely run up ahead; they're waiting for us just out of sight. Close your eyes late at night you may smell his musky odor, or perhaps hear his snuffle from the next room. Pay attention and you may feel his nose on your hand or back of your calf. When your final day comes, you can go on to meet him; he's never left you and never will, and when you close your eyes for the last time, you'll open them again to be met with his bright eyes and wagging tail.

Old dogs don't die, at least, not those dogs who take the biggest chunks of our hearts with them when they leave us. Those dogs are inextricably part of our souls, and they go with us wherever we are. Though we may not see them, we know they're there because our heart is still beating; we still breathe, and those of us who have been truly touched by a good dog know our lives really started the day we met them.

Magnificent dogs don't die. They shepherd our dreams and only allow the good ones through the gates of our consciousness. They watch over us much as they did in life, and that moment when we step just barely outside of death or disaster, it's because they moved our feet, or they stopped short in front of us as they did in life.

You see a good dog is something only given to a few people. They are a gift from the universe and, those there with us only a short time, they never really leave us. They are loyalty and love perfected, and once we are graced with that sort of love, we can never lose it. We merely lose sight of it for a time, and that is our fault; for how can a love like that ever go away?

It can't. It can't, and it never will. For these brave souls trade their hearts for ours, and they beat together beyond sickness, beyond death. They are ours, and we are theirs, for every sunrise and every sunset until the sun blazes its last, and we once again join the stars.

Memory Pages and Journal

In the following pages you can journal about your pet, attach treasured photos, plan a memorial, document signs you've seen and spiritual experiences you've had with your pet. You may also jot down notes from the chapters that inspire you, document ideas for a ritual or create the plans for an altar. You will find that these pages correspond to the chapters in the book and can provide you with a cathartic experience that will hasten the resolution of your grieving experience. The sky's the limit!

Memory Page (for your pet's photo
and date of transition, etc.)

Thoughts and Ideas from Chapter 1

Thoughts and Ideas from Chapter 2

_____
_____
_____
_____
_____
_____
_____
_____
_____
_____
_____
_____
_____
_____
_____
_____
_____
_____
_____
_____
_____
_____
_____
_____
_____
_____
_____

Thoughts and Ideas from Chapter 3

_____

_____

_____

_____

_____

_____

_____

_____

_____

_____

_____

_____

_____

_____

_____

_____

_____

_____

_____

_____

_____

_____

_____

_____

_____

Thoughts and Ideas from Chapter 4

Thoughts and Ideas from Chapter 5

_____
_____
_____
_____
_____
_____
_____
_____
_____
_____
_____
_____
_____
_____
_____
_____
_____
_____
_____
_____
_____
_____
_____
_____
_____
_____
_____
_____
_____

Thoughts and Ideas from Chapter 6

_____

_____

_____

_____

_____

_____

_____

_____

_____

_____

_____

_____

_____

_____

_____

_____

_____

_____

_____

_____

_____

_____

_____

_____

_____

_____

_____

_____

_____

_____

Thoughts and Ideas from Chapter 7

_____

_____

_____

_____

_____

_____

_____

_____

_____

_____

_____

_____

_____

_____

_____

_____

_____

_____

_____

_____

_____

_____

_____

_____

_____

_____

_____

_____

_____

Thoughts and Ideas from Chapter 8

_____

_____

_____

_____

_____

_____

_____

_____

_____

_____

_____

_____

_____

_____

_____

_____

_____

_____

_____

_____

_____

_____

_____

_____

_____

_____

_____

_____

_____

_____

Final Thoughts

_____
_____
_____
_____
_____
_____
_____
_____
_____
_____
_____
_____
_____
_____
_____
_____
_____
_____
_____
_____
_____
_____
_____
_____
_____
_____
_____
_____
_____
_____
_____
_____

Endnotes

Introduction
1   Swan, T. (2014). The Sculptor in the Sky. Bloomington, IN: AuthorHouse, LLC.

Chapter 1
2   Fantegrossi, D. (2019, March 25). "Why Losing A Dog Can Be Even More Painful Than The Death Of A Loved One." Retrieved May 9, 2020, from https://iheartdogs.com/why-losing-a-dog-can-be-even-more-painful-than-the-death-of-a-loved-one/.

Chapter 2
3   Nieburg, H. A., and Fischer, A. (1996). Martin Scot Kosins, "The Fourth Day." A foreword for the book Pet Loss: A Thoughtful Guide for Adults and Children. New York: HarperCollins.
4   Koontz, D. R. (2011). A Big Little Life: A Memoir of a Joyful Dog Named Trixie. New York: Bantam Books Trade Paperbacks.

Chapter 3
5   Kübler-Ross Elisabeth, and Byock, I. (2019). On Death and Dying: What the Dying Have to Teach Doctors, Nurses, Clergy & Their Own Families. NY, NY: Scribner.

6 Bach, R. (2001). Illusions: The Adventures of a Reluctant Messiah. London: Cornerstone.
7 Straub, M. B. (2019). Someone Else's Shoes: Walking the Muddy Path Toward Personal Sovereignty. Cardiff, CA: DreamSculpt Books and Media, an imprint of Waterside Productions.

Chapter 4
8 Kagan, A. (2014). Afterlife of Billy Fingers: How My Bad-Boy Brother Proved to Me There's Life After Death. London: Coronet.

Chapter 5
9 Swan, T. (2014). The Sculptor in the Sky. Bloomington, IN: AuthorHouse, LLC.
10 Abraham-Hicks material. (9/2018) (n.d.). Philadelphia, Pennsylvania.
11 Abraham-Hicks material. (9/2018) (n.d.). Philadelphia, Pennsylvania.
12 Robertson, B. (2015). Blair Robertson, Afterlife: 3 Easy Steps To Connecting And Communicating With Your Deceased Loved One. Tarland, Scotland: Aberdeenshire Publishing.
13 Coates, M. (2014). Communicating with Animals: How to Tune in with Them Intuitively. London, UK: Random House UK.
14 Hopler, W. (2018, May 3). "Afterlife Signs and Messages From Animals." Retrieved from https://www.learn-religions.com/afterlife-signs-and-messages-from-animals-124096.
15 Browne, S. (2010). All Pets Go to Heaven: The Spiritual Lives of the Pets We Love. London: Piatkus.

16 Hopler, W. (2018, May 3). "Afterlife Signs and Messages From Animals." Retrieved from https://www.learn-religions.com/afterlife-signs-and-messages-from-animals-124096.

17 Coates, M. (2014). Communicating with Animals: How to Tune in with Them Intuitively. London, UK: Random House UK.

18 Coates, M. (2014). Communicating with Animals: How to Tune in with Them Intuitively. London, UK: Random House UK.

Chapter 6

19 Trout, N. (2008). Tell Me Where it Hurts: A Day of Humor, Healing and Hope in My Life as an Animal Surgeon. New York, NY: Broadway Books.

20 Abraham-Hicksmaterial. (9/2018) (n.d.). Philadelphia, Pennsylvania.

21 Wigington, P. (2018, March 23). "Hold a Farewell Ritual for a Deceased Pet." Retrieved from https://www.learn-religions.com/pagan-pet-farewell-ritual-2561441

Chapter 7

22 Flannery, B. (2019, June 4). "Pet Sympathy Messages: Condolences for Loss of Dogs, Cats, and Other Pets." Retrieved from https://pethelpful.com/pet-ownership/Pet-Loss-Sympathy-Messages.

Chapter 8

23 Weiser, M. (2011, March). "Indians, Dogs Were Companions in Life and Death Centuries Ago." Seattle News.

24 Michie, D. (2017). Buddhism for Pet Lovers: Supporting Our Closest Companions Through Life and Death. Place of publication not identified: Conch Books.

25 Ichikawa, S. (2003). My Pig Amarillo. New York: Philomel Books.

26 Desy, P. lila. (2017, July 23). "Can We Communicate with Spirits of Deceased Pets?" Retrieved from https://www.learnreligions.com/communicating-with-dead-pets-1728720.

27 Tanaka, C. (2019, May). "Tokyo's Pet Loss Cafe Offers a Place to Grieve and Heal." Japan Times.

28 Epstein, Adam. "Pope Francis Says All Pets Go to Heaven, but What Do Other Religions Say?" Quartz. Quartz, December 12, 2014. https://qz.com/311346/pope-francis-says-all-pets-go-to-heaven-but-what-do-other-religions-say/.

29 Cook, Krista. "Will Pets Be Resurrected Along With All Living Things in Heaven?" Learn Religions. Learn Religions, June 25, 2019. https://www.learnreligions.com/pets-will-be-resurrected-3577545.

30 "Dogs in Faith and Fact." Dogs in Faith and Fact | TheDogPress.com. Accessed May 9, 2020. http://www.thedogpress.com/DogSense/dogs-in-faith-and-fact-Dr.19L12.asp.

Acknowledgements

The Pet Soul Book was manifested one faithful day after a meditation session. During that meditation, I received inspiration to write the book, and as a counselor, animal lover and someone who has experienced a lot of grief (both human and animal) in the past few years, I knew that I had a lot to share. I could provide support and assistance for anyone going through the grieving process with their beloved pets. I knew that part of the legacy of my life was to help others find peace as I had during the past few difficult years.

Inspiration for this book could not have been received without the love and support of the following much loved humans!

A special thank you, unending gratitude and love goes out to Gary, my husband, who offers me unconditional love every day, supports my crazy dog show lifestyle, and has learned to live and love a house full of six basset hounds. My loving family, my Mom and Dad, Pat and Jerry Timen, who love me unconditionally and have been supportive of everything through thick and thin. I am thankful that in the spring of the year 2020, my Dad is still

155

with me, though, my beloved mother transitioned in April. I feel like the writing of this book has helped to prepare me for her death and for the death of my beloved basset Cooper who transitioned from thyroid cancer four days before my Mom. My sister and best friend, Nancy: I am so blessed to be traveling through this life hand in hand with you. My sister Sally, who has passed into non-physical, who I know guides and loves me every day. My mother-in-law, Mary Moore (Mom Moore), who loves and encourages me daily. Special love and thanks also goes out to my special friend, spiritual soulmate and wife-in-law, MaryBob Straub, who has impacted my life in the most deep and profound ways. Thank you for the advice, encouragement and love along this authorship and life journey!

Also, deep thanks and gratitude to my dear, wonderful special friends, Tammy Gibson Dillard, my counselor and dear friend; Patti Banovich-Delashmutt, my oldest and dear friend; My Mastermind Group, MaryBob, Dr. Shawn Chou, Ruth Henry, Donna Shaw, and Tyler Joy White who provide unending inspiration and support. My girl's group, who while in the mountains of North Georgia helped to manifest this inspirational journey: MaryBob, Debe Boedicker, Kathy Prather, Melissa Thomas and Lara Rose Flanders. Thanks to my work-family at Zephyrhills High School, your constant support and love is so appreciated. Thanks to all of my friends in the Basset Hound, Great Dane and dog show world. I truly appreciate you all!

Very special gratitude and love goes out to my Dreamsculpt family, Publisher and Chief Executive Officer Lynn Kitchen who wrapped me up in a warm hug whenever I needed it. Her initial enthusiasm for my book project at the Dreambuilder Live seminar will be a moment I'll never forget! Editor and Chief Visionary Officer Jared Rosen, whose brilliance and inspiration helped guide and lead me through the journey of writing my first book every step of the way; and to Director of Artist Development Bill Scarcliff, my former husband and dear friend for continued love and encouragement throughout life and this project. Book designer, Darlene Swanson, who put the finishing touches on the cover. And a very special thanks to my fabulous cover illustrator Cheryl Caro.

For help and assistance with editing, thank you Catherine Astl, an author herself who generously agreed to lend her expertise!

I also want to express my thanks and gratitude to all of the folks who agreed to share their stories in the book. I couldn't have done it without your courageous storytelling, and I am forever grateful.

About the Author

Julie Moore, found herself stung by the experience of painful deaths of multiple family members both human and animal. Looking for a way to soften her own grieving process, she had the inspiration to write a book to soothe and guide herself and other pet owners who are deeply troubled by the physical loss of their beloved companions. With an M.A. in Counselor Education and Educational Leadership, and as a certified counselor she has spent the past 25 years guiding students to success as they prepare for adulthood. One source of Julie's joy is breeding and showing champion basset hounds under her kennel name ZephyrMoore Bassets. Julie is a lover of all things "dog", a cup of coffee on a porch overlooking mountain views, deep conversation with friends, great food and spending time with her husband, Gary and their 5 bassets hounds.

You can reach Julie through her website Thepetsoulbook.com or JulieMooreAuthor.com